This page is intentionally left blank.

© 2020

Kennon McLendon
Ospreys in Falconry
Cover photo: Christina Paz
Cover design: Christina Paz
Multiple interior photos: Christina Paz & Kennon McLendon
Book design: Daniel McLendon
Translation: Daniel McLendon

A CIP record for this book is available from the Library of Congress Cataloging-in-Publication Data

ISBN-13: 978-1-7355751-0-0

Ospreys in Falconry:
Lessons Learned

KENNON McLENDON

with KAKY & ANNA McLENDON

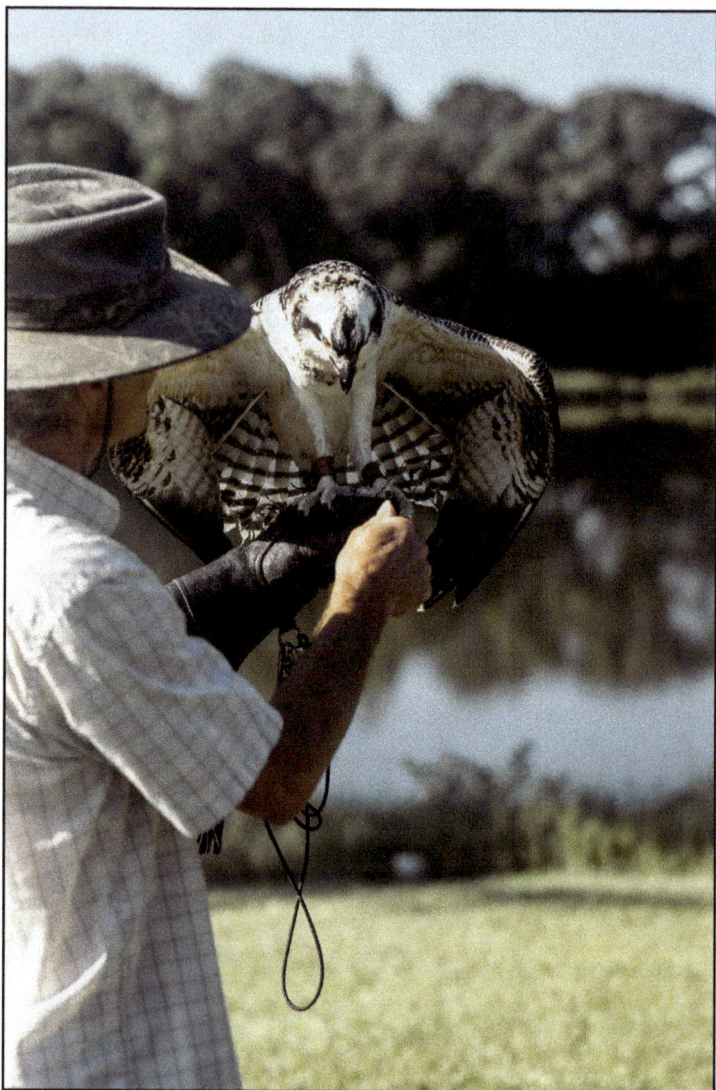

Photo by Christina Paz

Contents

PROLOGUE

The young osprey extends her neck, eyes fixed on the water. Her head bobs from side to side, performing a complicated calculus involving distance, light refraction, and prey size. Amber eyes glare at something invisible beneath the surface.

Suddenly her wings—black feathers trimmed in tan—pull up tight, prepared. With a final head-bob, she leans forward, launching downwards at a shallow angle, aiming straight for the water. Her eyes stay on target; her wings pump hard. At the last moment, she swings her legs forward, opens her talons wide, stretches her wings backwards, and plunges feet-first into the water. Eyes straight ahead, just behind her talons. She disappears in a tremendous splash.

Soon, a disheveled head pops up. She looks around, mouth agape, maneuvering to face the wind, then she flaps downward and pushes her tail into the water. Beads of water roll off her wings. She becomes airborne, barely, dragging a catfish in one foot. With the fish skipping on the surface and struggling to gain airspeed, she makes it off, flying straight ahead in ground effect. She pumps with effort and climbs.

At fifty feet above the surface, she shakes vigorously, losing a few meters altitude and shedding more water in her feathers; the lake beneath her shimmers with the miniature rain shower. She repositions the fish with her feet so it faces forward and she flaps steadily, trying to stay aloft long enough to find an updraft. The flapping stops as she noses into rising air. She circles slightly higher, wings aquiver as she banks or dips or floats, but soon she balloons upwards in victory, using lift against trees or thermals or bubbling puffs of wind.

At two hundred feet up, in a controlled soar, she looks back. She circles downward, makes two approaches in gusty conditions, then comes in fast, flaring with several forceful flaps at the last second. She lands upwind on her perch.

Right next to her admiring falconer.

He gives her a piece of fish to eat in exchange for her prey, which he secures. The osprey steps to his glove to finish the meal, one pair of talons half encircling his gloved wrist, the other deftly holding the catfish she eats—bones, spines and skin. She is breathless, panting between bites, wet and proud. The falconer walks her back to her mews.

The above scenario is the reason I'm writing this book. I've played my part in this scene many times, a scene many say is impossible. But it is possible; and I want to share my experiences with these magnificent birds as falconry partners. I have by no means perfected the art, and I expect others to improve on my methods. But I have proved that an osprey can belong on the arm of a falconer. What follows is an account of my journey.

One of 25 bream in a three-acre pond caught by this bird in stoops from various perches

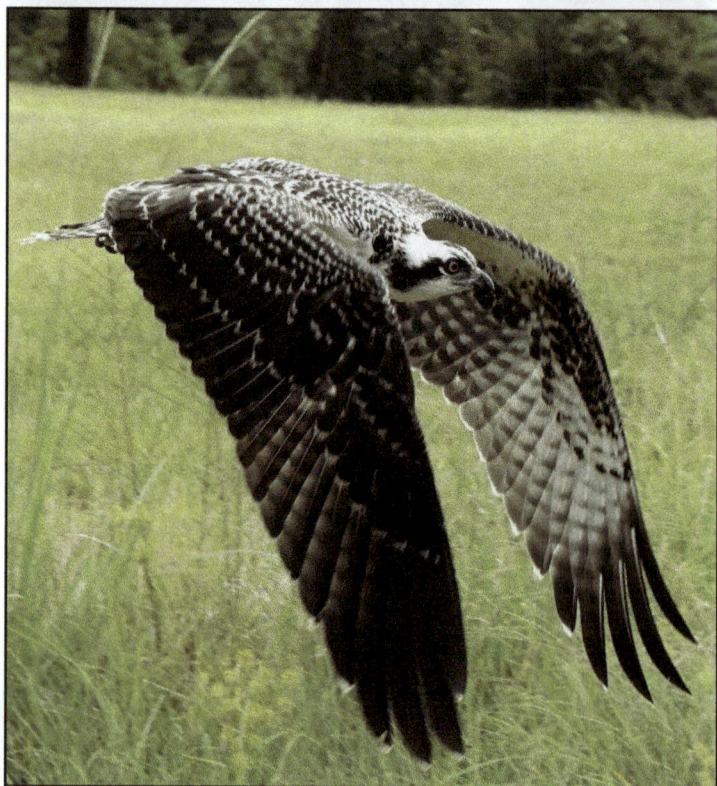

Falconry with Ospreys?

The first time my osprey caught a fish was a day to celebrate. I had been working with him for weeks—weeks I spent sitting next to a blue plastic kiddie pool in the backyard. His perch sat on the lip of this pool, which I had filled with murky pond water, while a bream swam in circles. He had snagged fish with this setup before, but that didn't count in my book. My goal was a successful dive on a free-swimming fish in the lake itself.

On this scorching July day, I passed over his pool perch and coaxed him onto his lakeside pole—a ten-foot PVC pipe with a perch on top. Once he'd adjusted, he began scanning the nearly opaque water of the pond. The pole leaned and swayed underneath him, but he didn't seem to mind.

I tossed a handful of floating fish food across the water. We had done this before, many a time, and he had tried to catch the slippery fish that bobbed below the surface. But so far, he had come up empty.

Suddenly, the pole swayed wildly as the osprey launched into the air. He splashed into the lake a few feet from the shore, into the soggy remains of the fish food. His feet went under and, for a second, his body rested on the surface; then he flapped his wings hard and lifted off the water.

I squinted, straining to see if he clasped a fish in his talons, not expecting much.

And there it was! His first fish!

I held my breath as he placed one foot in front of the other, streamlining the bream in his talons, holding it headfirst while he gained altitude. After circling back, his wings flared, and he landed with his prize on his home perch.

That was a good day. There are other days. This book describes both.

What is "Real" Falconry?

The less celebratory days remind me that ospreys and falconry are incompatible in many ways. Before I even got started, a host of commenters on social media warned me of the difficulties to come. Here are examples of a few comments :

- "Ospreys do poorly in captivity."
- "They are stupid."
- "They're untrainable."
- "How could you get them back?"
- "How can you catch one?"
- "They will migrate!"

Since I started, I've discovered even more reasons not to try it.

The naysayers have reasonable points, many being at least half-true. Ospreys are not easy birds to handle.

But even after I found an osprey, taught it to fish and return to my hand, and reported my results online, many questioned whether hunting with ospreys is real falconry.

The definition of "real" falconry varies, and no matter what your opinion of it, someone is always ready to criticize your activities. Carhawking for starlings with a kestrel, squirrel hawking with a red-tail, and catching ducks with a hybrid gyrfalcon are different enough from each other to generate group rivalry. The unkind folks may denigrate others as not being "true falconers." As for me, I just use a dictionary. Here's a simple definition:

Falconry is the taking of wild quarry in its natural state with birds of prey.

The quarry varies by raptor and geography. Furthermore, not all falconry quarry must be naturally occurring; introduced quarry is also valid. For example, "natural" prey includes Chukkar partridges under point by dogs in the western U.S. These birds are introduced and, under duress from the dogs, are not truly in their natural state. Even so, a peregrine snagging a partridge is "real" falconry by almost everyone's idea.

No man-made pond or lake has actual wild bass, but the introduced bass certainly behave like wild fish. That's close enough for me.

Sticklers may point out I'm cheating by using food to attract the fish to the surface. Point taken, but is using a dog to help a falcon catch a quail fair? Sure. More power to everyone!

My birds have stooped on fish they spotted while we were boating on the lake, and I say that's good sport. (Disclaimer: so far, their only boating catches have been fish chummed into position.) The ospreys have also caught several non-feeding fish within such tiny ponds that I'm not willing to call those fish "wild"; it's too easy.

Basically, any catch a pole fisherman considers legitimate is OK by me. So, the kiddie pool doesn't count. But a fish swimming free in a typical pond does.

One of my ospreys took twenty-five fish from a three-acre pond within a few months. That's consistent enough to qualify as "regular" prey. The dictionary definition doesn't specify catching prey regularly, but the ability to do so lends credibility to my endeavors.

So, with objections noted, I will henceforth use the term falconry to label what I'm doing, according to the dictionary definition.

Regardless, some will deny that my osprey activities are genuine falconry. To those I say, try it yourself! Improve on my methods. Definitions aside, I'm only trying to explore fresh territory with a magnificent bird. I invite you to do the same.

Why I Wrote This Book

I still haven't addressed the less philosophical objections, such as, "they're untrainable." I'll discuss these problems along the way; indeed, my journey will be full of them. But the reason this book exists is to document my experiments with these marvelous birds.

I'm not trying to say that they are for everyone, or even that they're great falconry birds, such as peregrines.

But I *am* saying, and will present my experience to prove, that you can keep an osprey healthy, hunt with them, and take part in the action, up close and personal.

Falconry with ospreys offers novel ways to interact with one of the world's most majestic birds. There are pros and cons to working with any bird of prey; I've been a falconer with the tried-and-true kestrels, red-tailed hawks, Cooper's hawks, and a peregrine, and "enjoyed" the quirks of them all. I've experimented with red-shouldered hawks and a barn owl. I've participated in the rehabbing of other species.

The osprey experience is just as rewarding as working with my other birds. But ospreys are, in their own special way, different. A falconer must make accommodations in husbandry, handling, and training.

With these accommodations, you can keep them healthy in a regular mews (I'll recommend a few perch ideas); transport them in giant hoods (these need extra tailoring); and hunt them. Or, should I say, *fish* them, for that is all they will catch. Well, aside from the rare accidental turtle, stick, or tennis ball.

Above all, keeping an osprey is rewarding. It's exciting when they come up with a fish! It's also entertaining to watch them soar, bathe, and dive, apparently for the fun of it. You can even get them to plunge into the water for a frozen fish "lure" if you want to give them a workout.

Throughout this book, I'll tell you everything I've learned. Though I'm certain I haven't found the best way to fly these birds, there is enough information here to enable a competent falconer to train an osprey to catch prey. I hope that others will come along and improve every aspect I describe.

I'm offering my experience in this hope: I want ospreys to get the recognition they deserve amongst falconers. For some, I hope they'll be a viable option when other birds may be less practical. For other falconers, who simply love these birds, I hope this work will persuade them that an osprey is not "impossible" or "just a pet."

In case you couldn't tell, I'm mostly in the osprey-lover category. They are gorgeous. Their overall outfit is worthy of kings' attire. They are majestic in flight. Their dive is a Blue Angel-style, high stakes, stunt; the showy splash at the end looks great on video. Their croaks, poses, feather-shaking, and head-bobs are endearingly comical.

Final Notes

Before you go any further, I'd like to address a few matters.

First, some of you may disapprove of any anthropomorphizing I do. It's a dangerous thing, but please indulge me. This is the fastest shortcut to convey what I've learned about my birds' personalities. You must understand some personality traits to handle and train these birds. (For example, their fastidiousness relating to their feet makes creance flying difficult.) I also make some overly broad generalizations.

In addition, please recognize that this book is not an academic paper on the viability of ospreys as falconry birds. For most of the book, I'll be matter-of-factly direct, but I'm not attempting to be scientifically precise. At the risk of over-generalizing, and for the sake of readability, I intend to use empirical language over scientific.

On a related point, I want to emphasize again that I'm relating my own work with ospreys and my interpretation of that experience. My sample size is limited. Overall, my personal experiment is certainly not up to scientific standards. If you see problems with my conclusions, I encourage you to get an osprey yourself and see if you can't solve them.

With all that said, thank you for picking up this book. I hope it will reveal an undiscovered world.

Common names: *fish hawk, river hawk, mullet hawk, eagle hawk*
Order: Accipitriformes, which includes hawks and eagles
Family: Pandionidae
Subspecies:
1. Pandion haliaetus carolinensis
2. P.h. haliaetus
3. P.h. ridgwayi
4. P.h. cristatus

- P.h. carolinensis breed in North America.
- P.h. haliaetus are found in Europe, northern Asia, the UK east to Japan, and from Russia to the Mediterranean and the Gulf of Arabia.
- P.h. ridgwayi breed in the Caribbean.
- P.h. cristatus are found in Australia and the Pacific Islands.
- Ospreys are protected under the Migratory Bird Treaty Act.

PART I: CHALLENGES

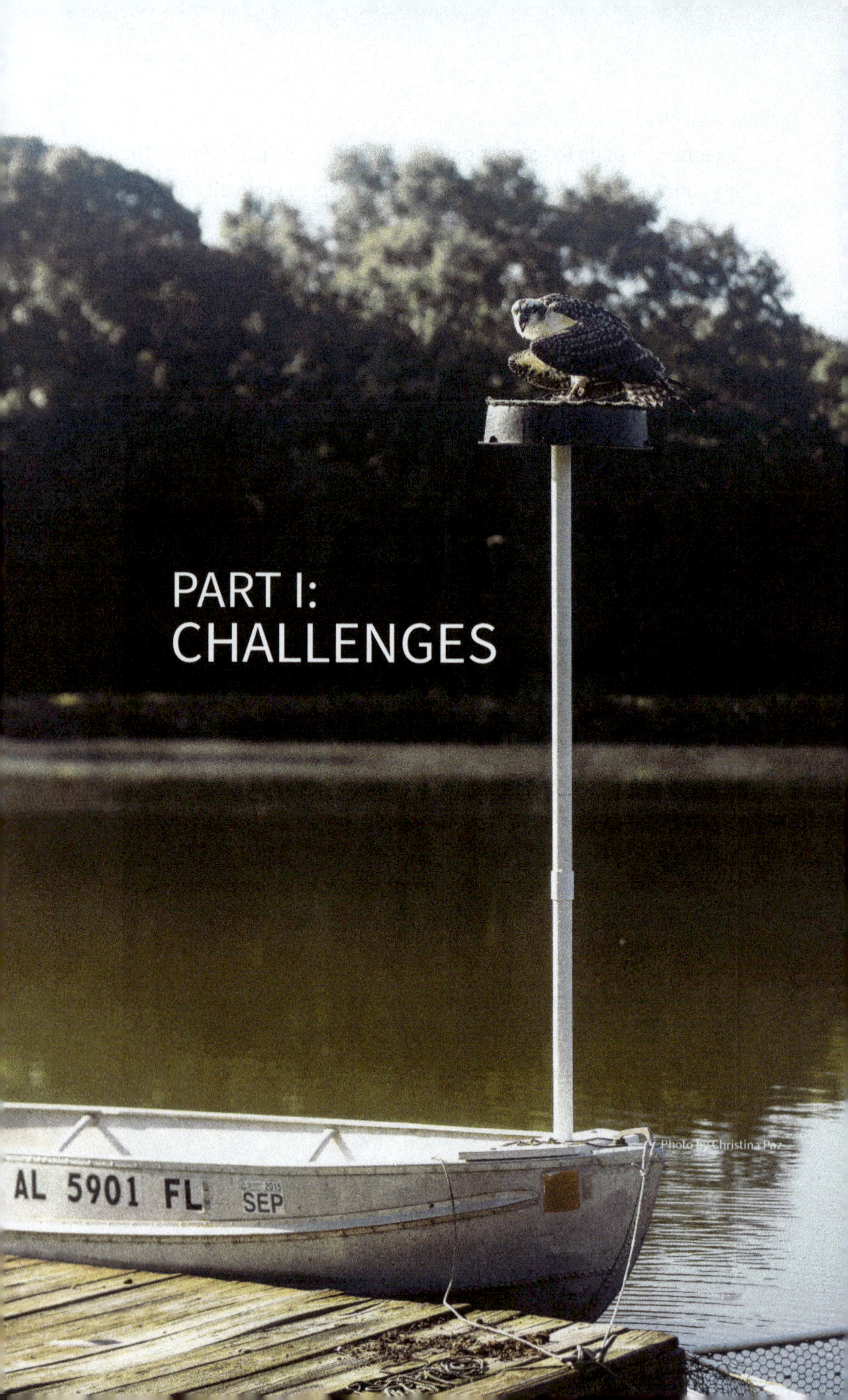

Photo by Christina Paz

The Cautious Raptor

So, what is an osprey's temperament like? These birds will strike any falconer as a little unusual.

Despite the large size and fearsome appearance, ospreys are not very bold. They are like a slow-motion accipiter: nervous about a sudden attack and anxious in conditions that make them vulnerable. Unlike the typical accipiter, most of what they do is with hesitation, with many false starts. Occasional panic attacks. Perpetual concern about what's out there. Except for those moments when they dive, they are never oblivious to danger, and it shows. Ospreys are cautious concerning the current situation and any potential change in situation; their anxiety encompasses both the present and the future.

This wariness is reasonable, considering their always-exposed environment to weather and avian predators—the lurking, prey-snatching bald eagles—and several potential water/prey complications. (Is the lake too shallow? Are the fish too deep? Too big?). Not to mention the nests they're raised in: naked, exposed structures which give them no place to hide.

Now, the red-tail, for example, shows concern regarding predators and competition, but she's not usually nervous. She's the Terminator. *I see food! Attack, since I am in control. What? Raccoon? Break off engagement, fly to a nice perch, rouse a little, and scan for squirrels.* (I saw this happen!)

Contrasted with this rough and tumble, "first responder red-tail," ospreys are circumspect and timid.

Don't misunderstand, once they have decided to dive, they are lightning fast off the starting line. They will tackle fish that are too big to fly with and swim back to shore with them, if it comes to it. They'll even fight a coyote. (That story comes later.)

But they think and rethink. They take time coming to tidbits. They may wait until the red-shouldered hawk flies away. The falconer's new hat may slow their return. They deliberate before leaving a perch and don't leave swiftly, unless they have an excellent reason to do so. (One excellent reason: Fish!)

An osprey may look around and check their feet several times before launching. They evaluate the wind and flight path at length before committing. They pinpoint a target fish's depth in the water, proximity to obstructions, size, and who knows what else, bobbing their heads at the water for an excruciatingly long time as they gather more visual data.

Even once they make it into the air, they often change their minds about a dive or a landing. But they can't simply change it "on-the-fly" as another bird might; they start back from scratch. While a red-tail makes a last-millisecond swerve to a better perch, the osprey aborts his landing completely, circling the entire pond before attempting again.

I mentioned accipiter. The Cooper's hawk, for example, is hypervigilant and easily spooked. Sudden death could emerge from a bush a meter away. Or it could be a feast? No time to decide! Fly fast! They are flying away before you can hear the sound that startled them. They are diving into a bush after a bird you never saw. Always hypervigilant. Always murderous. Always fast.

Ospreys share the hypervigilance, but at a much slower pace. You can see echoes of the wide-eyed, manic Cooper's glare, but it presents itself in over-caution, rather than flightiness.

Ospreys dislike being crowded by towering trees. They aren't fond of bushes or branches dangling overhead. They prefer wide-open spaces with plenty of room to maneuver. That said, they can get used to other environments; once accustomed to a confined area, they will fly to it. Usually.

Cooper's calm their mania by catching and devouring prey. Their motto? "Food First!" Ospreys, on the other hand, want a routine perch and their own piece of land with a lake view—a controlled environment. Ambience matters more to them than food.

Ospreys' Attitude to Food

In fact, the osprey's relatively uninterested approach to food causes a few issues in falconry.

Imagine you are an osprey, and you catch a fish miles out to sea. You secure the catch and begin a long flight home. With only water for miles around, you must be on high alert, watching for robbers. You can't eat while flying; you can't even think about it until stable on a perch.

For ospreys, a disconnect exists between catching and eating. Redtails delay slightly while they decide where to eat. With Cooper's, the delay is even shorter. But ospreys are slow to eat. Everything must be perfect first.

Just examining the eating style of an osprey versus the red-tail is illustrative. Red-tails eat with gusto, after a brief survey for danger or a little mantling. It's easy for them to connect catching and eating. In contrast, ospreys eat long after the catch. Once they start, they gingerly handle the bones and spines they pack into their crop. They prefer to begin at the lips; this technique ensures they can eat the whole fish. If they start at the tail, gripping becomes more of a problem with the last few bites.

I'm suspicious they prefer to let their prey die before feeding. I've seen them perch with a fresh catch for several minutes before eating, just waiting. It's possible that gnawing at the mouth of a razor-toothed Spanish Mackerel might have survival consequences; so, it's not entirely unreasonable for them to have that instinct.

To summarize: their desire for food does not drive out fear as quickly as other raptors, which slows training. They ruminate over multiple factors before they act, even with a tidbit right in front of them. An osprey falconer needs a great deal of patience.

Physical Differences

As ospreys are exclusively fish-eaters, important differences in physical capabilities affect falconry practice. While they're powerful and elegant in wide-open skies, the same qualities that make them suited for wind and water get in their way in traditional falconry exercises.

Although their legs can snag a heavy fish, they don't hop well and must fully fly to reach a perch only a few inches higher. (I suppose you can't hop out of the water.) They can't nimbly return to a perch or glove if they're tethered.

Once they make it onto a glove, their inch-long, two-forward, two-back talons tend towards the "sticky" side, meaning that they may have trouble releasing their grip. They sometimes have difficulty distinguishing the glove from the fish when trying to leave the glove.

Overall, their flight is clumsy in tight quarters. The same unique wing joint that enables them to plunge another few inches into the water makes comfortable flitting around a mews impossible. They can't maneuver in a small area with one flap of the wings. Even the smallest change in perch requires full-wing deployment and flap-

- As of 2019 there were an estimated 50,000 breeding pairs worldwide, plus 25,000 – 30,000 non-breeders
- 70% of ospreys are found in Sweden and eastern regions of North America
- 5000 pairs live in Florida, with densest populations nesting on a few south-central lakes. On Lake Istokpoga, which has about 300 pairs, ospreys nest in cypress trees with two to three nests per tree.
- The Red Sea contains two-thirds of the Middle East's ospreys.
- North America has the largest osprey group in the world, of which all migrate except those in the south – about 25,000 – 30,000 pairs. This is two-thirds of the world's ospreys.
- About half of North America's ospreys are found in Canada.

No real hooding problems. Steve Tait 24 fit Ozzie well.

ping. There is no hop up to the fist; there is no half-fly. There is only full-wing deployment, flying or walking. It's helpful if you think of the osprey's capabilities like a sailplane — excelling and graceful in the open skies but lacking the maneuverability of a shorter winged aerobatic plane. Not designed for forested areas or compact spaces, they may bump into objects other raptors would dodge, or avoid landing in areas that other birds find inviting.

There is one other similarity to accipiters that bears mentioning: they are hard on tail feathers. Osprey clumsiness coupled with stiff tail feathers seems to be the cause. My first osprey broke the tips of several tail feathers once, after I tried to put him in a hood I had in my redtail supplies. I set him on his perch successfully, but after I closed the door on him, I heard a lot of bashing noises. I opened the door to find him stuck behind his perch, with the aforementioned broken feathers.

To summarize, ospreys are clumsy on the glove, in the mews, and with a tether. As these are the mainstays of "real" falconry, it's not so surprising that falconers have dismissed them in the past. But these challenges are just that—challenges to be overcome.

I'll describe in detail my experiences, successes, and failures with three ospreys, bird by bird, over three years. I'll also throw in any other helpful information I've learned.

PART II: THE BIRDS

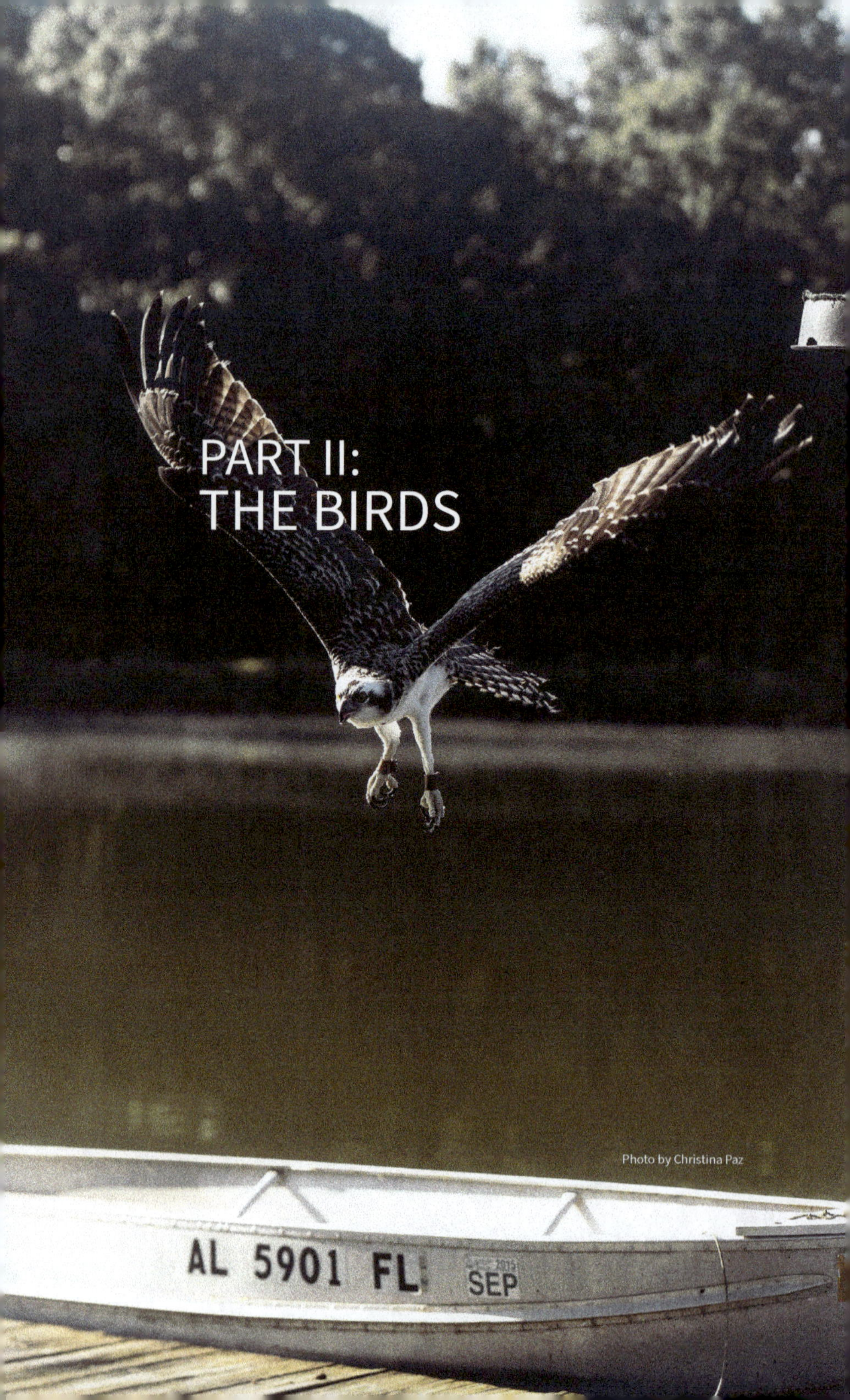

Photo by Christina Paz

Bird One: Oscar

Ospreys are captivating birds. I had often seen them around my house and on coastal fishing trips, and I began thinking about the possibilities. I was already a falconer; I had ponds, fish, equipment, space, and patience. It wasn't an orthodox choice, but I decided to give ospreys a shot. I hoped a little flexibility might offer the key to success.

I was nervous using an osprey for falconry since these are mostly uncharted waters. Before I started, I read everything I could find on the subject. There wasn't much.

I found the story of Neptune on the internet. (It's translated in the appendix and worth a read.) I studied lots of material from rehabbers, who reported that ospreys were fragile and difficult to raise successfully. Falconers agreed. The online falconry community's outlook on ospreys was, to summarize, "No!"

Still, as the stubborn, skeptical sort, I detected no definite deal-breakers. Obstacles, certainly, but none of them insurmountable. Many of the horror stories about "fragile" ospreys started with injured birds, so maybe healthy birds would be sturdier. Red-tailed hawks, now considered an obvious choice, were only recently discovered to be impressive falconry birds. In considering the details, and weighing the pros and cons, I decided to go for it.

I watched a video of someone feeding an eager osprey chick; it didn't look too hard to get one to eat. Procuring enough fish to feed one was a common complaint in the stories I read, but three ponds surround my house, and my wife and I are fond of fishing. I was confident I could keep it from starving.

Lots of fish and the upside-down bathmat which seemed important for traction

With some imagination, I envisioned ways to capture a passage bird, and I saw easy ways to obtain a chick. I considered anklets, tethering ideas, perches, boats, and so on.

After emailing the head of the U.S. Department of Natural Resources, I got it in writing that ospreys, specifically, were legal to use in falconry. (I had read the rules, but they're difficult to understand. And it just *felt* illegal.)

Since I never heard a definite "not possible," I went for it.

Having spent decades on the water in various recreational activities, I noticed the increasing numbers of osprey nests blossoming on the top of almost every suitable navigation marker, radio tower, piling, or dead tree—an encouraging sign, given their population decline in the last century. With their rebound looking secure, I wasn't too nervous to keep an osprey from a conservationist viewpoint. It's likely that taking one chick from a clutch would actually increase the chances of the others surviving. In other species, the high death rate of young birds in the wild makes falconers a relative non-risk, from a bird population standpoint.

I was a master falconer and had experienced success with other birds. Besides birds, I've had numerous pets my whole life (some more traditional than others). I had enough money to see it through and building skills to make the necessary equipment, and, overall, I am a reasonably competent person. A college degree in biology helped my confidence, if nothing else. All that to say, I concluded it would not be irresponsible of me to capture and raise an osprey for the sake of falconry

But all the naysaying wasn't without effect; much of it was reasonable. So, I decided to get a late eyass—the equivalent of a brancher

- Eyries can last hundreds or thousands of years.
- Male ospreys collect branches for the nest while females provide grass, moss, and bark.
- Nine out of ten osprey pairs will choose a man-made structure for a nest site.
- Eyries can be 13 feet high and as large as a double bed.

in other raptors. (With ospreys, there are frequently no branches around a nest; they prefer poles, or dead trees with wide views.)

At this stage—about seven weeks—the birds clutch the edge of the nest pile and flap their wings energetically while holding themselves down with their talons. They're flying enough to escape gravity and learn some control, often lifting on wind gusts, but they're still secured to the nest. Since the nests often sit over water, their first true flight needs to be pretty competent. Usually, they can't simply land on the ground nearby for mom to bring food.

I chose to capture a bird in this stage because a fully-fledged, flight-capable nestling would have a better chance of surviving husbandry. It would also have a better chance of successfully migrating if it became separated from me.

I already had a mews I thought would work, and I had lots of equipment lying around from the various birds I had trained over the years. Now, with a copy of the DNR email and my falconry license in hand, I set out to get the first bird.

Raising the Eyass

June 4th. I recruited my long-suffering wife, giving her only need-to-know information. The two of us set out on the one-hour drive to the lake nearby.

In tow, we had an old, 22-foot Grady-White offshore boat with a hard top. I brought an aluminum ladder in case the nests were out of reach, but I was hoping we could get to a lower nest if I stood on top of the boat. We had all the normal raptor-trapping supplies for protecting the bird and myself. We had electronic charts to prove the location of the nest (legal implications) and lots of heavy clothing and a softish broom for self-defense.

In the end, the broom wasn't necessary. Although I expected sudden, searing neck pain at any moment, it never came. The mother only circled above us, calling with concern, while I approached. I stood on top of the bobbing boat, while my wife stood capably at the controls.

On tiptoes, I could just see into the nest. That was the first time I smelled osprey. It's like nothing else. A kind of aromatic, pungent, chemical odor. My wife finds it unpleasant, but to me, it's only odd.

Three nestlings, indistinguishable from each other and all staring at me, were squeezed into the meter-wide nest. Fully feathered, they looked as scary and large as any red-tail I had dealt with.

I took both hands off any support (never a good idea on a boat) and grabbed the closest bird. Right hand grabbing the upper legs, spreading them between two fingers. Left hand reaching under and supporting the chest. I nimbly fell back onto the boat, making sure that if it was a bad fall, I would be injured first, like a mother protecting her newborn. My landing was just graceful enough to be safe.

In my grasp, the bird felt strong and capable, and I was soon covered in flailing wings. I scampered down, completely forgetting to confirm the bird had all its wings, eyes, legs, etc. (I once tried to train a red-tail that only had one eye. It didn't work. See appendix II for that story.)

Using my typical red-tail handling, I got the baby bundled up in a box. I didn't hood him or use stockings but laid him in a cooler with smooth insides, ventilation holes, and towels. He didn't fight or act unusual, just frightened, as one would expect.

After the longest boat ride ever, checking on the baby every few minutes, we got back to the dock. We offloaded him to the air-conditioned truck, hooked up the boat, and headed out. My wife pulled the trailer home, as I was busy working with the bird.

He was frightened but not alarmingly so. Right away, he took some torn fish from tweezers. Yay! I didn't know if I'd gotten the starving runt or the spoiled eldest. It wouldn't have been easy for the parents to feed themselves and three huge babies. But this one ate one full-grown bream that day.

I placed him inside the mews in a round tub, elevated about two feet. The roof on my osprey mews is partly slatted (for weathering) and partly solid (for protection). I felt confident he could float down from the elevated tub if he desired, but he showed no interest in doing anything but surveying his surroundings and eating and slicing.

The next day the baby ate two large bream. I offered pulled pieces of the entire fish to him with tweezers or fingers, and he ate with no hesitation. By the third day of this diet, he weighed 1238 g as a fed-up, full-cropped, fat baby.

I keep saying "he," but I have no idea of the gender, even to this day. The male/female dimorphism overlaps in ospreys, so there was no easy way for me to tell. But we named him "Oscar," and from then on, he was "he."

Oscar perched on my glove that third day, and I weighed him and put on anklets; it went the same way it would with other birds, except that he pecked a little more vigorously, with a painful twisting motion. He didn't try to foot me but acted fearful, like a just-trapped juvenile red-tail. He would step to the glove, but if he bated, he made no attempt to regain his footing. Even after he tamed down, he couldn't fly back to the glove after bating without a lot of help. He rarely even tried to return to the fist. He also rarely bated while being carried, but when he did, I helped him like I would a newly trapped red-tail—by gently cradling him back onto the glove.

In a week's time, he ate well on the glove, in his nest box, or on the floor. I fed him a full crop of one to two bream per day. He was able to tear up a whole fish and self-feed, thank goodness—hand-feeding is slow. Still shy, he only stepped up on the glove when I presented it to him closely. With his weight around 1000 g, he didn't act hungry unless his crop was empty and it was late afternoon.

Oscar perches on the nest box.

Osprey Falconry

It was June 25th, twenty-one days after capture, before he flew to my glove across the mews. On July 5th, a full month after bringing him home, he was flying predictably to a 50-meter creance.

Oscar never became accustomed to the jesses and always inspected them before takeoff. And he didn't like the pull of a creance at all. Though I've used the same techniques with my other birds, none have been so offended by leg restraint. (My other birds were Cooper's hawk, American kestrel, red-tailed hawk, red-shouldered hawk, barn owl, barred owl, and peregrine falcon). He flew free better than he flew on the creance.

At 950 g to 1000 g, he would fly to the glove for a whole fish but demur at a tidbit. Numerous free flights, weight trials, and perches near the water indicated that at these weights he would return to the glove if his crop was empty. The precise weight didn't matter much.

Oscar flew vigorously but never soared. I used his nest box as a training perch. This was a plastic feed tub attached to a larger upside-down feed tub—a light, portable, washable, durable perch. It was green, easy to spot, and easy to become accustomed to. He seemed to consider it his home, and it was his most reliable return point.

The bird screamed frequently. Almost constantly, unless he was scoping something out. Sometimes he gave a loud peep, like "I'm here!" Other times, it was a definite "Bring me food!" I had tried to prevent the screaming by keeping him well-fed as a baby, but I clearly failed.

On Aug 6th, two months into the experiment, he flew from a pond-side, high perch (three meters) and snagged a frozen fish I had thrown into the water. He circled and landed on his nest box positioned in the middle of the back yard. He didn't seem interested in landing on my outstretched glove while he was carrying his fish.

For the next several weeks, I flew him at many dead fish presented in different scenarios: floating, submerged, from the glove, from

25

the perch, and from a canoe. He occasionally dove at live ones; I fed bream while he watched, and he dove when they made their quick grab of the floating flood. But he had no successful catches of live fish.

After he caught a dead fish, he always circled back to his box.

Until…

Trouble

The first sign of trouble occurred when a couple of friends came over to see the bird. Oscar was mild-mannered with his feet but quick to peck, and he screamed almost incessantly.

I let him fly off to his perch. He had no leather on him at all, not even anklets because I thought they might interfere with fishing, and I wanted him to perform his best in front of the sightseers. I was used to flying him without leather; he balked at being tethered to a glove, and my combination mews/weathering pen didn't require outside tethering. So, I had no reason to put anklets on him. Other than the obvious.

After he landed on his perch, I moved about seventy-five meters away with my friends. When I whistled and flashed the fish, he flew towards me but veered off before landing on my outstretched glove.

Oscar flew around in a wide circle, and the wind blew him further and further away until… he was gone.

Whistling didn't bring him back. My property is divided by ponds with no direct route to his last location; I had to take the long way around. I jumped in my car with my glove and a fish in hand and took off in search of him.

I zipped over the back roads which surround the property. Once I arrived where I had seen him last, I slowed down, opened the windows, and began to whistle persistently. The road cut the clearest path between the trees, so it was no great surprise when I heard him whistle back.

Not surprising, but certainly welcome. He was perched on the top of a telephone pole. The only clue that he wasn't a wild bird is that he looked at me as he called.

He flew to the fish in my hand without hesitation this time; maybe he was more willing since the scary friends were gone. I settled him down to eat on my glove, and we sat together in the front seat of the car as I drove back to the farm one-handed.

He behaved fairly well on the way, but I did slide the seat all the way back to give him room. Upon our return home, he went back into the mews as if nothing unusual had happened.

More Trouble

The second sign of trouble was a little more obvious.

He simply flew off.

On Oct 18th, he left his perch, circled moderately high in a weak updraft, made it just over the trees on the south side of the pond, and disappeared.

He weighed 930 g. Despite the lower weight, he wasn't interested in the fish I displayed as soon as I sensed trouble. He looked vigorous and healthy with strong wingbeats. I'd seen nothing that might have spooked him.

- Three weeks after the first flight, the mother migrates while the father stays behind and continues to feed the osprey chicks.
- At five to six weeks after the first flight, young ospreys are ready to migrate (at 11 – 12 weeks old); shortly after that, maybe even a day later, the father will also leave.
- It can take a migrating young bird two to three years to find a nest and a mate.
- The Amazon basin hosts 60,000 – 70,000 migrating American ospreys annually.
- During peak migration in October, bird watchers in the Florida Keys will see up to 400 a day.
- Ospreys can fly 2500 – 3500 miles (4000 – 5600 km) in four to five weeks.
- European ospreys reach their final stop—West Africa—in about 38 – 40 days; 22 – 26 of those days are actual flying.
- One in three European ospreys die while crossing the Sahara.
- One osprey flew from Finland to South Africa—a 6,000-mile trip.
- It's unknown where ospreys go during migration from Japan, Russia, and Eastern Europe.

But many days of driving around whistling and searching proved fruitless. He never came back.

Well, maybe he did: I was suspicious of a couple of ospreys that passed by our house for a visit the next spring. Was it Oscar, with a new partner? If it was, he showed no interest in coming back to me.

Observations

Here are some things I learned with this bird:

On the negative side: He left. I took Oscar as a late nestling which, perhaps, impaired his ability to survive on his own. He never caught a live fish that I saw.

Clearly, I didn't have solid control of him. Although lowering his weight might improve this and get a rapid response to the glove, I was afraid a sharp condition might be dangerous since I was well-aware of ospreys' reported fragility.

On the positive side: He left healthy and able to dive and bring back a fish (albeit dead) from under water. This gave him a good chance of catching a live one when he got hungry enough. He was a very late nestling, more like a brancher, so he should have been sociable with his own kind, with all the basic survival skills. I achieved a level of control—something to celebrate when dealing with a so-called untrainable bird; he returned reliably with his baggy catches to a nest box where I could retrieve him.

And, of course, I learned a lot about the idiosyncrasies of ospreys. And I thought I could do better with the tail feathers next time.

So, what else did I learn from my first osprey?

It's easier to obtain an osprey nestling than that of most other species used in falconry, if you know when and where to go. Nests are present in numerous publicly accessible lands (i.e. waters). You need access to a boat and the coordination to retrieve one from the nest.

At least this nestling ate ravenously, appeared content in his mews, and flew well to the glove. Hunting wasn't quite successful, but dives on staged prey made this seem achievable, given more time. I retrieved the bird by using a preferred, habitual eating perch. From a falconry perspective, he had potential.

He ate a ton of fish. I typically fed him one bream on one day and two the next. I would also feed him larger fish, when I managed to catch one; a foot-long catfish seemed to fill him.

Oscar pecked and screamed annoyingly but showed no hint of footing (which would have been painful and problematic).

He had great difficulty recovering perches after bating, with significant risk to tail feathers. He couldn't travel in the traditional giant hoods. Anklets and jesses were issues. Traditional tethering as a whole was tricky.

He had a fragile tail and a unique odor, which I assume is a result of his waterproofing oil. His liquidy mutes smelled strong, and he could slice this slurry up to ten feet away.

A homebody, Oscar liked to eat in one place. He had a highly nervous disposition. He flew readily for a whole meal but not tidbits.

He flew away.

But there's always next year.

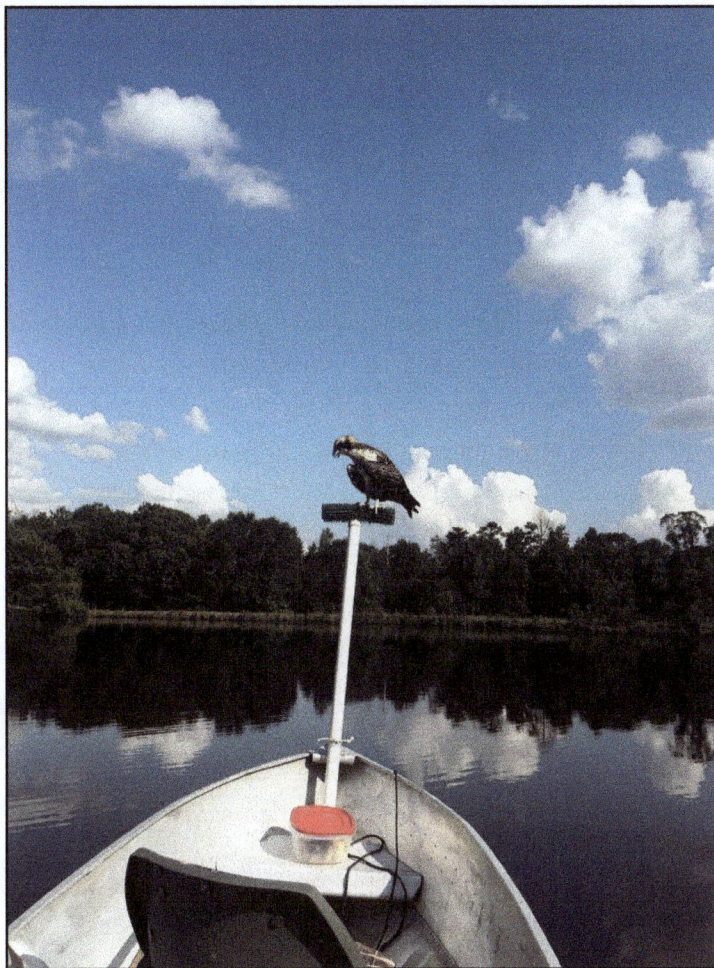

Opie scanning for fish. The size and depth of the fish have to be just right. Sometimes it's a sudden stoop, sometimes a long, drawn out, head bobbing decision.

Bird Two: Opie

Before I launch into bird two, I just want to reiterate that you must consider osprey falconry with somewhat fresh eyes. Success may look a little different from, say, catching fifty squirrels in a season with a redtail. My hunting with a barn owl is also a little different, but no failure in my eyes. (Look for "Alex" in the appendix.)

My point is this: as far as I'm concerned, osprey fishing is successful falconry. The bird in the story I'm about to tell caught twenty-five bream free-swimming in a three-acre pond. I was able to retrieve him (sometimes smoothly, sometimes not) after all of these kills. The prey may be cold-blooded little fish and not birds or mammals, but the stoops and soars were magnificent and just as exciting to me as other falconry experiences.

Enough already! Onward to Bird Two.

Raising the Eyass, Round Two

May 9th. Note that I started three weeks earlier in the year this time, aiming for a younger bird. Since keeping the first bird healthy was not a problem, I was willing to try a younger one, hoping it would be easier to train. On this date, the nestling would be about a month old. The nests around here seem to develop simultaneously, so I expected to have a choice of several nests of similarly aged nestlings.

My mews. The slatted bottom handled the mutes well. Notice the impressive amount and distance covered. The perch is a grounding rod inserted into a drilled board onto which the pan is mounted.

Most baby raptors do not survive the first year, although ospreys do better with 40%-50% surviving. So, as I mentioned before, I wasn't worried about harming the population myself, nor did I feel that I was causing excessive risk to the life of an individual bird.

So, on May 9th, more confident in the whole proceeding, we towed the Grady-White to the lake, with a falconry friend along for the ride. We left the broom and ladder at home this time.

The day was uneventful, as far as it goes; everything went as planned. I (legally) snatched a baby from the same nest as last year, with the mother circling and scolding overhead. Once again, three babies filled the nest! I remembered to make sure the nestling had both eyes, but I didn't have time to scrutinize the nestlings to pick the smallest, which was my original plan. For conservation reasons, I would have liked to take the runt; but I saw no obvious difference between them.

This eyass still had visible down puffing out between his tan-tipped black feathers. Proper feathers fully covered him, but the flight feathers were just sprouting. He stared at me, mouth agape, peeping. A somewhat big-chick peep, but still some version of baby babble.

Opie greedily accepted torn or chopped whole fish from the start. He ate them, bones, scales, and gills. I assume he needed the calcium. He would cough and shake out anything too hard to swallow with comical vigor.

At first, he ate a full-size bream a day, then two to three per day. I bassinetted him around in tubs and towels and laps and fed him constantly. He soon ate fish chunks straight out of an old margarine tub. He wobbled when he stood but mostly sat around.

Young Opie after a bath. The water-resistant nostrils are apparent. My birds have the trachea somewhat to the side of the esophagus. I first thought this was pathological!

I washed him daily—a necessity, what with the liquid mutes in a contained space. I kept him indoors, using less and less restrictive tubs until he finally sat in a low padded pan inside a plastic-lined baby pen.

I was surprised by the amount of floating down he emitted. This had repeatedly surprised me in the past with other birds, but some things are hard to learn. White bits of fluff began to fill the house, so I rigged up a standard air conditioning filter in a big plastic box with openings and a fan to catch most of the strays. This evolved to a square fan with a filter taped to one side. A small vacuum cleaned the filter and the playpen of feathers, when needed. Towels trapped the mutes on the bottom and sides. The whole design smelled slightly and occupied a central position in our living room. This setup wasn't universally accepted.

- In the middle ages, "keepers" tied baby ospreys to trees. Their parents would deliver fish to them which the keepers would take away to eat.
- In the U.S. in the early 1900's, ospreys paired up in large colonies; they nested in trees or on the ground.
- From 1950-1970, DDT use killed eggs, and populations plummeted—in some areas as much as 90%.
- After the DDT ban, ospreys began nesting on artificial sites.
- Nests are found on cliffs, manmade platforms/poles, buoys, power poles, cell towers, cacti and even house roofs. On small islands, they will nest on the ground.

Relative Success

The highest weight in the next few weeks was 1240 g. After he began standing, I would carry him around on the glove. After his feathers grew in, he began flapping his wings hard while clutching the ground or his perch, practicing. Soon it became clear he was actually holding himself down. From there, he practiced flying with vertical hops lasting about a second. On day thirty-two, June 10th, he flew right up to the roof of the house.

I was a little spooked by this sudden development, but he came down at once to an offered fish and landed beside me. He acted nervous about attempting a direct landing on the glove. Once he started flying daily, his weight dropped, and with a daily full crop, he stabilized around 1000 g.

I never flew him on a creance. I initially flew him late in the evening when the chances of him soaring away were low. He was attentive but not desperate. If I offered him small tidbits, he might not come. A bigger chunk, and he came. Around this time, I discovered that a towel clip lanyarded to the glove was essential for holding onto slippery fish.

I started him on live prey by putting bream in a wading pool. On first sight, he flew into the six-inches of water in the round, blue plastic pool and trapped the fast swimming fish after three or four attempts. He showed no hesitation but clearly realized he had to act fast.

I had set up a perch for him next to the real pond as well—a PVC T pipe slid over a stake. I hammered this into the bank of the pond, with enough height that he could look over a broad swathe of water. I could also move this perch and secure it to the bow of a small boat. In the end, he preferred the perch on the boat—as long as the boat was ashore!

On July 8th, he stooped for a fish in the real pond, with the traditional splash. He returned to his perch immediately but didn't dive again. After this, he dove on feeding fish almost daily but never connected.

On July 25th, Opie caught a musk turtle, giving said turtle a once-in-a-lifetime parasailing experience before dropping him back into the lake.

On July 30th, after dozens of dives from the T perch, he came up out of the water with a real fish. He flew around more than usual and chose to land in the nest box I'd set up in the yard; he chose the box, instead of the T perch or my glove (which was attached to a whistling falconer). At least he was happy to let me approach. I secured the fish and picked them up together. After several minutes of gripping the fish, scanning everything around (and above), and checking his fish repeatedly, he began to eat.

He repeated this performance twenty-four more times over the course of the rest of that year, catching the twenty-fifth in the middle of December.

Though moving the boat always made him nervous, he usually hunted from the bow or the perch on the bank. He never caught one from the moving boat, but he made several stoops from it. His catches decreased in number in the colder weather, as the fish quit showing up.

If he caught a fish, I retrieved it by giving him a fleshy hunk too big to swallow. He would release his fish, using his talons to hold the tidbit.

He never returned to me directly with a catch; I had to fetch him from wherever he settled with it, typically his perch. But he also never flew into a tree. He did sometimes land out in a pasture across the pond, eating his fish on the ground, periodically screaming and scanning.

This set up kept the house clean for a short while.

Even with the incessant food availability as a baby, Opie screamed a lot. Sitting on his perch, he would scream until a potential target appeared. Then he got quiet, stretched his neck, and bobbed his head. If he decided against a stoop, he began a somewhat routine scream. After a few unsuccessful attempts, or if the fish didn't come to feed (fish are a mystery), he begged. He faced me or any hapless passerby (including the dog), dropped and shook his wings like a tiny baby wren, and screamed for food.

Every once in a while, he stooped less dramatically than usual and took a bath while floating in the pond. He dipped his head and shook his wings, as if in a bird bath, bobbing in the water and generally looking non-predatorial.

An interesting thing happened on November 8th, fish twenty-four. After a routine catch, the bad bird landed across the pond in a pasture, behind a clump of trees. As I watched him land from across the water, I saw a flicker of movement nearby, which soon materialized into a coyote racing from the trees towards Opie.

All I could see between the leaves were lots of wings flapping (like my palpitations!) and gray blurs; but before I could develop a plan, the bird took off, landing in the middle of the pond, exhausted. After he made a half-hearted, failed attempt to take off from the water, I jumped into the canoe for a retrieval.

The fish and coyote were long gone. I couldn't find any injuries on the osprey, though, and he ate well afterwards.

That was the peak of excitement for fall and winter. Opie willingly dove in 42-degree weather, but my southern fish were lying low, and catches became uncommon.

The following spring, he made some impressive soars on windy days, up, I guess, a thousand feet. He responded to my whistles, but he descended in calculated increments, always circumspect.

Tragedy

At this time I had a male redtail named "Sora." He was an athletic bird, flapping straight up to the tops of trees and diving down trunks in his pursuit of squirrels. I didn't have to coax him to chase them; he caught one on his second free-flight and continued to catch them thereafter. Sora proved to be an exciting hunter compared to most of my others, with lots of catches in rapid-fire attacks or on squirrels bailing from trees.

Sora was also an opportunistic, stalking, fearless killer. I had witnessed this twice—once, he killed a fully grown peacock. (See the appendix II for that story.)

On this day, Opie was feeding up in his mews. I remember thinking, *I wish he wouldn't eat so close to the side. A raccoon could grab him*. But the thought wasn't strong enough to spur me to action.

Turning my attention to other birds, I took the redtail out for a hunt. He followed me around the pond as I stirred up squirrels, in our usual routine. He got high in the trees and, in typical fashion, spotted something quickly. I maneuvered around, ready to help him, trying to spook whatever squirrel he saw back to his side of the tree. I was excited as he took off.

But to my dismay, he headed across the pond towards the mews. Impending doom fell over me as I realized what his target was.

Opie. Still feeding next to his slatted weathering pen.

I started my 400-yard dash. Smack. Sora was plastered against the side of the mews.

By the time I arrived, Sora had bound tight, both talons sunk into the osprey's chest. The redtail held on to the osprey through the slats, his wings flat against the vertical boards of the mews. The osprey was motionless, pulled up against the inside of the wall by the hawk. Using tidbits, I tried to persuade Sora to let go. I tried scaring him, I tried squeezing his head, but he held fast.

I went into the osprey mews and pulled out each of the redtail's talons one by one, pushing away Sora's continued attempts at binding, and somehow avoiding getting footed myself.

Opie didn't look good. He had mortal wounds. He was quiet. Limp. Soon, he was dead.

Falconry is a roller coaster. I still remember my peregrine, Pierre, exuberantly stooping, blazing across the farm from a high pitch at something I couldn't see. He, too, had been killed by a redtail, though a wild one.

I've had a Cooper's hawk die on me and a kestrel that flew off. And, of course, my previous osprey had flown away.

Studying and practicing falconry prepares you for loss. Sad things happen with "normal" falconry birds, even when the falconer follows all the tried-and-true advice. But the loss was especially hard for me to bear because I didn't feel the long falconry tradition behind me regarding ospreys.

But despite my sadness, I was closer to achieving my goals with the second bird compared to the first. I learned some things from Opie, and I'll list them below.

Observations

- It's possible to catch free-swimming fish with an osprey in a fashion similar to an accipiter dashing after a spooked rabbit.

- It's possible to keep them healthy and flying.

- It's possible to keep the stiff tails intact with careful handling and perch design.

- Multiple perches or perches near walls are not good. Central perches with lots of wing space are essential.

- In my experience, ospreys are not footy, but they like to peck.

- You can retrieve them after a catch, but carrying is a significant issue.

- They bathe floating in ponds.

- A short, solid wall around the bottom of the weathering pen is a really good idea.

Bird Three: Ozzie

The next year, more confident of our husbandry, we set out again even earlier. With accipiters, many say "the younger the better." On April 18th, almost a month earlier than the last bird, we headed to the lake once more with our probably reliable boat.

Same nest as the prior two years. Same drill. But this time, they were just tiny chicks! I scooped up one of the three in both hands and stumbled back onto the boat.

This one reminded me of the frail game bird chicks I've incubated and brooded. He must have been less than a week old, with a light tan head and undersides, and dark facial trim and topsides. A light streak ran down the middle of his back; his dull little claws and curved bill were merely hints of things to come.

I needed to keep him warm. Since it was a balmy day, he probably would have been fine in the box on the way home. But I got nervous about chilling him, so I nestled him in my shirt.

An hour later, back at the house, the little tan bird squatted on a bed of towels in a plastic container, warmed by a heating pad beneath the towels. He peeped and swallowed the first pieces of fish torn off for him.

The initial weight was 98 g. A good bit less than the 1400 g he weighed later. I say "he," but that's just a guess, based on his weight.

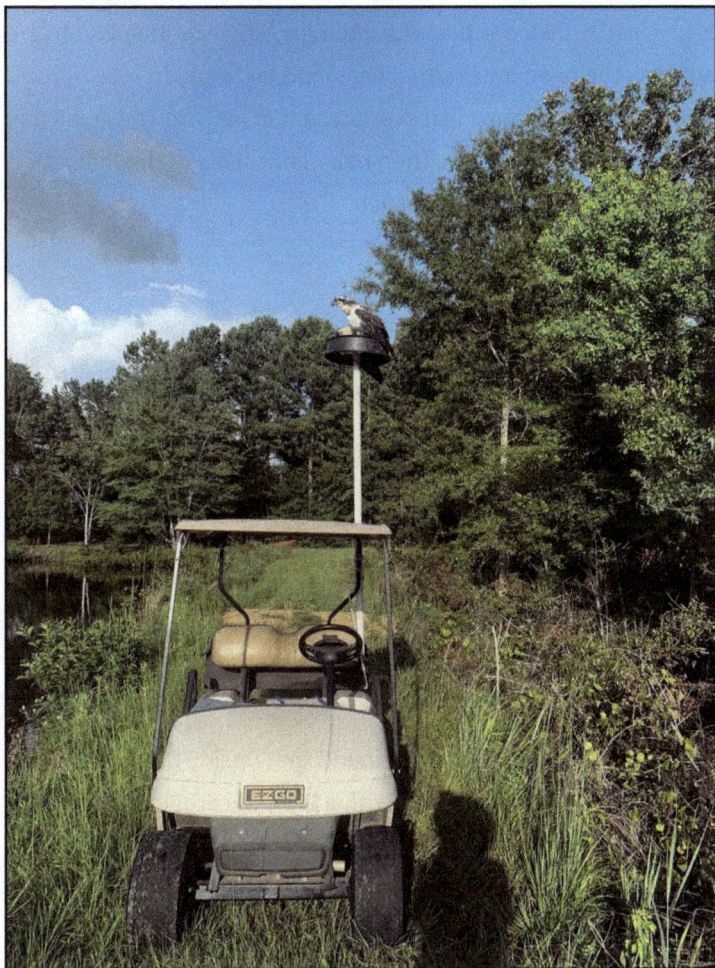

Ozzie would hunt from a very slowly moving cart, but any wobble, or if we got too close to a tree he didn't like and he was off. He would return and land but usually only if the cart was stationary.

Reported weights for genders vary, so I'm not certain. There's good reason to expect smaller birds in the southern U.S. since several different raptors up north tend to be heavier.

He gained the rest of the weight—fourteen times his initial measurement—within a few weeks. Using tweezers, I offered him bits of fish sprinkled with raptor vitamins, which he greedily ate. He outgrew the need for external heat, and he began to feed himself from a pile of chopped fish ever present in his box. The small box gave way to larger boxes, then baby pens. Lots of down floating around, lots of mutes. Lots of fish.

I got blisters chopping and tearing fish to pieces with scissors. Desperate, I tried a food processor, but the resulting combination of slurry and large chunks were difficult to deal with. I had yet to discover that tin snips help tremendously, being strong enough to easily cut through the bigger bones and scales. Later, I also learned that a guillotine-style paper-cutter was nice for a change of pace but only for small or scale-less fish.

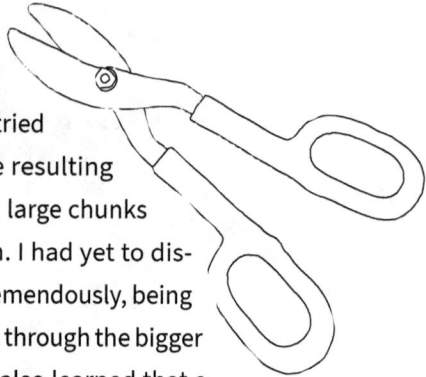

To prevent spraddle legs, I found that upside down bathmats worked well. The cheap kind, with a layer of carpet and a layer of squishy grip on the bottom. They were the right combination of soft and sticky, so he could keep his legs in position when squatting and when learning to stand. The mat carpeting itself, underneath the gummy layer, helped to absorb liquids. The entire thing could be hosed down and set to dry in the sun. I had a three-day rotation of these.

I was elated when he finally ripped up and ate his own fish unassisted by my tired, blistered hands. My family life significantly improved when I moved him outside, but everyone missed him a little.

I set him up in a large, flat tub with the inverted bathmats inside the mews. After he got a few feathers and sturdier legs, I raised this tub a couple of feet. He shot his mutes well away, whitewashing the mews walls. I kept him stocked with fish, always available in increasingly larger tubs.

I took him out daily, hosed off any mutes on his tail, and let him sun. Ozzie was a nice, gentle, huge chick.

Before his feathers filled in, he began exercising his wings regularly, stretching them, and later flapping about the yard or while on his perch. With the feathers came flight, first pulling against gravity as he tethered himself down with his talons (scary, big, and sharp), then actually flying as he loosened himself from the earth.

As soon as he could fly, he came well to the glove. At this stage, he roamed around the backyard, and I introduced him to fish in various situations: on my glove, on the ground, or swimming in the pond.

Learning to Fish

This time, I got something more sophisticated than the blue kiddie pool: a low, plastic water trough. I mounted a wooden/artificial turf perch along one side. I ultimately planned to place it in the mews as a perch, with several fish swimming in it so he would have food for a couple of days.

He hesitated to jump in, at first. He wouldn't fly to the fish when they nestled along the sides because he wanted to avoid injuring himself.

After several days, he learned to pounce on the fish and fly with them up to the perch. It took him about five wingbeats to go ten

47

inches (this is one wingbeat for a red-tailed hawk!). He now had all the basic elements for hunting.

At this point, I knew the trough would work as a self-feeder, but I never used it in this manner.

After this success, I put him on a high perch next to the dock on the pond, but no fish came to food. This didn't shock me, because they had been coming less and less recently, despite my regular feeding. At least thirty turtles showed up, though, and the bird head-bobbed at them.

I decided to transport the bird in the wooden box to other ponds. Since this osprey was less nervous than the others, and I had captured him at an earlier age, I attempted another giant hood. I got him in well enough, but within a few seconds, he lost the perch and lay spread-eagled in the back of the box. The wing feathers were OK, but he had broken the last inch of several tail feathers. I was especially irritated because I knew this would happen.

The good news is that the failure of the giant hood approach forced me to use a regular hood on him. The hood calmed him while he sat on a perch. I hadn't tried this before, since I only planned to hunt him near the house, but he was moderately easy to hood and tolerated it well. He ducked and dodged a bit, but the hardest part was getting it over his gaping beak—a clever defense. A size 24 Steve Tait worked perfectly. I tested several of these, because my dogs chewed up two of them ($69 a piece, on sale) before I learned to put them away more carefully.

In our hunt for fish, I shuttled Ozzie around to the different ponds on our property using a low perch set on the back of a golf cart. The temperature stayed close to 100° F for most of the summer, so this cart was a welcome luxury, handily carrying perches, fish food, me, and Ozzie.

I got some great action camera shots, but he had yet to catch a fish. At one site, he repeatedly dove where the bream were bedding over several days, but he couldn't connect with the quick and wary bream in foot-deep water.

Occasionally, I walked along the dam, the bird hooded on the fist. Then I'd unhood him when I spotted the shadow of a fish. But no catches. These fish were facing us and, with the sun and resulting shadows, spooked too soon. Regardless, he would dive for them, so successful hunting stoops direct from the fist looked possible.

Now my supply of fish became a problem. Typically, I fished from the ponds to supply the osprey with his regular meals. I always put a few live fish back in cages so I would have a meal ready for him even if I forgot to thaw one from my frozen stash. Unfortunately, the bream fishing slacked off.

I tested and fertilized the ponds—good for the long-term, of course, but as the water got healthier, it got murkier. Ozzie hesitated to stoop into the opaque water.

So, I decided to take a trip to my dad's—an hour and a half drive—where he has a pond full of bream. The hooded osprey sat in the back of my mini-wagon and behaved well. Towels draped everywhere caught most mutes on the round trip. He didn't scream the whole time; he sat still.

My dad's fish refused to cooperate, too. "Wrong time of day," Dad said. "They feed in the afternoon."

Still, Ozzie made several stoops and showed a willingness to return to his tall perch either staked to the ground or mounted to my dad's Gator ATV. He circled a few times before he returned, indicating nervousness, but he came readily to the glove after an unsuccessful splash. We went home with no catches.

Destination Fishing

Several more days of misses at home preceded another trip to Dad's. This time, I intended to carry him there in a small airplane. I can fly my old bush plane from my pasture to my dad's in twenty minutes—a much more efficient trip than the drive.

This time I tried a giant hood design, which I used in combination with a regular hood. It was basically an upside-down box; crude, but it worked. (Note: I have a few useful details about this contraption and other equipment collected later in the book.)

At three thousand feet, it was still hot. The plane bumped on the thermals, and I doubted that my wife, in the passenger seat, was happy.

After arriving at my Dad's farm, everything worked smoothly. I got him out of the box and on the glove easily. A few gates and a Gator ride later, I stood beside the pond, sweating in the ninety-degree weather. My wife, mother, father, and nephew watched nearby, hoping for something interesting to happen, though their definition of interesting probably differed from mine.

The wind favored an upwind landing; the perch set up was OK. *That big green and white truck might look scary on his approach to landing...*

I got Ozzie out from his new hood smoothly and approached the bank. The fish began stirring, and Ozzie fixed on them. I had planned for him to see the action, get moderately interested, and fly up to the perch specially made for portable deployment after the plane trip. Instead, he dove off my fist into water twenty feet away.

He came up with a fish. His first fish! A nice bream. And my wife got a video! I was thrilled.

I was less than happy when he didn't return on his first circling, but that was typical. He shied away from the truck, as predicted. He did the usual osprey post-catch behavior of circling several times before a return.

I became truly unhappy when I saw him circle and drift further away. While I whistled loudly, he banked around a stand of trees.

I ran toward his last location, calling and listening for his calls. Nothing. I hopped in the Gator and sped to likely landing sites in various pastures, stopping frequently to listen. Nothing.

I joined my dad in his truck and left the farm. We drove slowly with windows down, stopping frequently, looking up with binoculars, searching through the surrounding neighborhoods. (A few curious stares at our odd behavior.) Nothing.

Idiot. You have a telemetry setup you could have used on him. He wasn't even particularly hungry. You knew the truck would be scary. You got him as a nestling. He's not ready to be on his own. He'll never find his way home from here. I was really getting upset.

I drove back to Dad's farm, continuing to periodically call. Some crows were making a racket, and I hoped they might find him for me, but their caws lacked urgency. I stood in the clearing surrounded by

Osprey taking a bath in the pond. It's like a normal bathing bird, only they are afloat. They can also drink on the wing.

tall trees, and I glimpsed a possible raptor. Just another vulture or redtail? I'd been fooled before. My heart didn't pound until I heard the crows get excited. Soon I saw Ozzie soaring around, with crows in pursuit, talons now empty after his private meal.

He immediately recognized me and circled down. I held a big, fat piece of catfish he could see from a hundred yards. He began his final approach, then slightly veered. I started to worry, but it soon became clear he was simply correcting for the wind. He landed on my glove like always and started eating the fish. His crop was full, but not tight—about what I would expect from an adult bream.

Still a bit nervous, I prepared to grab him if he startled, since he had no jesses on. But he showed no indication of wanting to leave my glove.

The rest of the outing was uneventful. I repackaged the osprey into the plane and we all flew home. My landing was a little rough, but the preceding flight was smooth. (If mama's happy, everybody's happy.) The bird remained in good shape. But I needed more fish.

Migration

I mentioned earlier that being a falconer prepares you for loss. While the end of my time with Ozzie is less tragic than with Opie, this last bit of the story holds important insights into using ospreys in falconry. It touches on one of the big potential problems: migration.

About a week after he caught his bream, Ozzie left.

It was late September, the typical migration month for ospreys. He was behaving normally but wasn't hunting as aggressively as I would have liked. I started dropping his weight, feeding him one eight-inch catfish a day for two days. On the third day, I provided a bigger meal — and that's where the story begins.

His weight was 1350 g. In the past, he had returned well in this range. I wasn't expecting trouble.

Confident that the hunting part of falconry was a proven enterprise, I determined to do something new: I'd figure out how to handle these birds.

Maybe this one would be different, I thought. I would try longer and harder. I wanted to be more mobile and controlled and, hopefully, pave the way for more traditional handling of ospreys. Future falconers need to know how to restrain these birds, and perhaps I could discover some tricks.

So, I measured, made, and placed removable anklets on him. He disliked all of this, and despite being hooded, pecked me relentlessly, even twisting off a small chunk of my skin for the first time.

I tethered him to the glove and unhooded him. He sat calmly, then tried to fly off as usual, but the new tethering stopped him. He bated a lot—worse than a newly caught red-tail. Twice he regained the glove with a measure of control, and I thought he was making progress. But it didn't seem to stick with him, and I had to lift him back to the glove for many bates afterwards.

If he turned his head toward me, and I touched his upper legs as I lifted him with my right hand, he would settle well onto the glove. Other times, he instantly bated.

I tethered him with the anklets to a low perch in a shaded spot of his yard. He would bate, lie prostrate for a few minutes, and finally stand up on the grass. He never bothered to fly back to the perch.

After manning and hunting passage Cooper's hawks, I wasn't inexperienced with nervous birds. But his progress was slower than a Cooper's in regaining gloves or perches.

Time came for his afternoon hunt. *Maybe I should try him in the mews or not fly him free after such a morning exercise.*

I approached his perch where he was weathering. He'd been fairly quiet all morning, but now, after my lunch, he whistled at me in recognition, wanting food.

The above thought returned, saying "Stop," but the voice was too quiet, as I removed his restraints and his anklets for the daily hunt.

He sat on the glove normally as I aimed him towards his regular perch. After a minute, he flew off straight for the water.

He took a skimming drink and flew a couple hundred yards straight away, only turning as he reached the woods. He turned and circled.

As he circled higher with determined, deep wingbeats, I sensed that hunting was not on his mind. He was leaving. With animated gestures, I offered a big half catfish, something he'd never refused before, but I could tell he wasn't interested.

He flew around wider and higher and then directly overhead, looking down at me a few times. For once, I was hoping to hear his shrill screeching, but his strange silence signaled his independence.

On about the eighth circuit, he started drifting in the light breeze, searching for lift. He soon found it and circled over the trees to the south, out of sight.

I, of course, was whistling and waving the fish frantically.

After a few minutes, I headed out in the car to scan any possible perches or likely landing spots. I broadened my search to the surrounding neighborhoods, the ones within flying distance given the time he'd been gone.

I persisted and drove for miles, following the river south, but I spotted nothing on the ground or in the air. Several days of searching and calling were fruitless.

All that winter, I saw his empty, lonely perch waiting for him down by the pond.

The following spring, a pair of ospreys flew over checking us out as I checked them out. Neither looked precisely like Ozzie, and they moved on without ever appearing the least bit tame, never seeming to notice the fish I was holding out.

Later, a lone osprey came by and hunted the ponds, stooping occasionally. I ran to the freezer to get a fish, just in case. He flew close and hung around in the air for quite a while; he may have been Ozzie, but he didn't come to whistles or a fish.

While losing Ozzie was a blow, I know he has as good a chance or better than most juveniles of surviving (although he may have difficulties socializing with other ospreys).

If I get another chance, I'll take greater pains to keep my bird from migrating. I'll be more alert to the bird's perceived offenses in my handling. Probably, I'll keep him in the mews for the high-risk weeks in the late summer. I'll try harder with telemetry.

And I'll keep a fish in the freezer for Ozzie.

Observations

After bird three, what now have we learned?

- Ozzie's successful fishing wasn't a fluke (almost a pun).

- Younger nestlings can be raised and are less spooky than the more mature ones.

- Carrying is a problem, but returns with a full crop are the rule. (Though that may be a little presumptuous, given the way I lost him.)

- Hoods are possible.

- A giant hood will work to protect the hooded Osprey and the interior of your vehicle.

- Ospreys will dive to bathe or apparently play. They will also dive at leaves or tennis balls.

This style boat is great for access to nests on the shorter navigation posts. This particular boat was great when it wasn't getting repaired.

- A fish "lure" maneuvered in the water attracts them immediately, and you could give them a good workout if you are quick enough.

- They can drink on the wing at fast flight speeds after dropping low and flat to the water. It happens quickly, and the bird often follows it up with another approach, dive, and floating bath.

- They can swim a hundred yards, but this is tiring for them.

- Migration is most likely an issue.

PART III:
KEEPING OSPREYS

A young hatchling within ten days of hatching and young enough to need brooding.

Opie just out of the nest. He's probably ready to eat.

Well, I hope you learned something from my osprey stories. I was a little reluctant to be so open about my failures, but my purpose is to further the knowledge of these birds in relation to falconry.

I've learned several practical details that might not have been apparent in the narrative, so the rest of the book will be a sort of "how-to" guide. I'm going to change things up and give blow by blow recommendations organized chronologically, from eyass to successful hunting bird.

I wouldn't dream of trying to rehash all that a falconer needs to know. I'll just try to highlight aspects of osprey care and handling that are distinctive from typical falconry birds. If you noticed that I skipped a major step, that's because I used the same tried-and-true methods I'd use on other birds.

I'll state the overall disclaimer that my (and, perhaps, everyone else's) experience with ospreys is limited. Someone out there surely knows more, but I can't find a book that lays out such information.

We are early in the exploration of these beautiful birds and their capabilities in the sport of falconry. I've come up with one way of hunting ospreys, but more than likely, other methods work just as well.

Ospreys are not stupid, but they differ from the typical falconry bird. Their intelligence is distinct enough that we need to decipher a few things. Cracking their "code" seems tantalizingly close.

I'll assume that anyone still interested either loves ospreys, rehabs them, or is a falconer with ideas swirling around. For brevity's sake, I'll use falconry lingo.

Ideas for Keeping Ospreys

Obtaining a Bird

In the southeastern U.S., osprey nests are everywhere. The large public lakes created by dammed rivers have lots of marine marker posts with accessible nests on them. A hard T-top boat works great for reaching them.

You can't see the babies until they grow some, because the little ones are hidden by the sides of the nest. Mid-April may be favorable for finding them in the Southeast, but I recommend a scouting trip.

I have trap design ideas for a passage osprey that should work (which means, I've never tried them). But I would expect older birds to be tricky to handle, in the same vein as the passage accipiters. Due to the likelihood of trouble with them, I won't trap a flying osprey anytime soon, unless it's one of my own birds that doesn't return as planned.

The Eyass

For raising the eyass, you'll want an assortment of tubs in various sizes with a soft, but friction-providing surface in the bottom. Initially, a towel is good, if you fluff it up and shape it to hold the tiny bird. But as it gets more mobile, transition to upside-down bathroom rugs.

You want the carpeted kind rather than foam, and make sure to get one with a sticky bottom for grip. This bottom layer of grip gives good friction so the bird can "stand" on his haunches without developing splayed legs. The underlying carpet layer provides enough padding that the bird can lie down comfortably. Overall, they are a convenient, durable, and cheap way to provide grip and cushion.

I've seen no ill effects from using bath rugs, but stray fibers from the "human" side of the carpeted mat occasionally pull through, and I worry about the bird ingesting it or trapping a talon.

Heat lamps, reptile mats, overhead brooders, or other arrangements are necessary for warmth. Ospreys will gape if too hot and shiver if too cold. They will typically peep when they're unhappy about the temperature.

I set my nest containers on a kennel mat which produced heat to about 85° F within a climate-controlled room. I attached a reptile mat to the side, which made a contact surface of about 110°F with a towel layer separating it from the bird.

For the first two weeks, the babies will flatten themselves against the towel contacting the hotter reptile heater. They start gradually moving away from this source and by four weeks, they seem most comfortable with no heat beyond the kennel mat.

My thermal camera recorded temperatures just over 100° F on their heads and torsos near the legs. The backs were considerably cooler.

The babies eat a lot relative to their size. They and their appetite grow dramatically, with visible daily progress. You must start hoarding whole fish early in this process so you can chop or tear it up later for the baby. Tearing the fish may prevent a possible injury to the crop with bones, but the birds seem capable of dealing with sharp pieces, even at a young age. I myself was careful with long and bony pieces, but I did give them bones because I feel sure the calcium is necessary. (Fish with scales might help with calcium, too.) I also used raptor vitamins the first couple of weeks.

Chopping a whole fish into edible chunks is an increasingly onerous task. Game shears and tin snips are very helpful in preparing the fish. I used a paper cutter (the guillotine, office type), and it was nice for a change of pace but probably not worth the money to buy new. If you run across a used, heavy-duty cutter, I'd pick one up.

Manning and exposure should proceed as is typical with other young eyasses. Aside from the increasingly large tubs they'll live in, you'll need an assortment of plastic tubs to carry them everywhere you go. The rapid growth will have you changing tub sizes often.

Ospreys slice their mutes far and wide, so a typical falcon setup won't keep the house clean as the baby grows. Mutes are smelly and liquid, as well. I tried baby pens, kennel panels, and plastic sheeting with various degrees of success.

All of those options have pros and cons, and I choose which one based on weather, space in the house, other pets, etc. The mutes are even more trouble than an adult redtail's, so be ready.

The shedded down is something to contend with. One trick I use is to tape a household furnace filter to an electric fan. You can find them in many sizes and the most common sizes can be easily and efficiently matched to a square fan. If you place this near the eyass container, it'll vacuum up lots of feather debris, keeping it out of the rest of the room.

When you care for the bird inside, you'll have the mess of droppings and the downy dust storm that comes with new feathers. By far, the easiest way to keep a clean house is to get the bird outside as soon as possible, temperature and feather growth permitting.

Once I move them into the mews, I provide a warm, low-walled container. A heated kennel pad and a much smaller reptile enclosure heating pad rest on top of my elevated, slatted mews floor. A large tub lined with the upside-down bath rug lies on top of that.

Only slightly different from my inside arrangement, this setup keeps the overall bottom at around 85° F, with a small area at 100° F. The bird adjusts his temperature by flattening out on the part of the floor that feels best. In case of extreme or inclement weather, I have heat lamps available, as well as the "Great Indoors."

Food

Whole fish is their exclusive diet, and ospreys will eat bones, scales, spines, every last bit. Sometimes, they may drop a small piece of smelly entrail, or if the fish is particularly large, they won't eat the skull or skeleton, but as a rule, they leave nothing behind.

They eat slowly and methodically. While a fish with ribs and spines surely is hazardous, I've encountered no problems from bones, scales, or sharp gill covers. They protect themselves by careful positioning of bones before they swallow or by vigorous head slinging or coughing to remove anything objectionable.

Rarely, they'll produce pellets. I've seen only one in several years; it contained some fish backbone, grass, and fibers from the bath rugs.

Ospreys pause a long time before eating and don't eat as greedily as other raptors, so feed them well before dark once they've entered the mews.

They eat loads of fish; I'll give exact numbers and weights later on. Bream and foot-long catfish are a convenient size, but still lots of work to process. I've fed them cut up chunks of huge sailcats and five-pound bass (several days' worth of meals each). They eat about two small bream or a foot-long catfish a day without getting too fat. This will, of course, vary with the temperature.

In the Mews

I'm sure there are better ways to go about this, but the following set-up has worked well enough for me. The mews is a 10' by 10' slatted wood structure, half covered in tin with a slatted wooden floor. Inside is a large (16" diameter) central round perch atop a small post set through the floor. An upside-down feed pan covered in soft artificial turf works well for the perch.

Since the roof is only half-solid, the perch is partly exposed to the elements. In the wild, these birds have little shelter. My birds don't hesitate to hop around on the floor of the mews; if they're miserable on the perch, they can escape.

Don't forget the legally required large bath pan. I've never seen my birds use them, but they also get near-daily dunkings and frequently bathe in the ponds. I see them fly low and apparently wash their feet, skimming across the pond. Sometimes, they appear to take flying sips of water.

In my experience, multiple perches increase the chance of feather damage. The more poles are protruding from the floor, the more likely they are to back against them, breaking tails.

Ospreys must fully fly to gain even a low perch. Because of their need to extend their wings to get on or off, they bump into any wall-mounted perches; thus, my perch in the center of the area. If the perch is too high, they hit the roof before landing.

Maybe a bigger mews would be nice for more perch choice, but it would have to be very large, since ospreys can't maneuver well near walls or objects.

I suspect a smooth floor (though not too slippery) is helpful. The birds like to walk around drooping their wings just enough for the primaries to hit the floor, which might cause wear if the floor is rough. Regular factory-sanded deck lumber for human feet works fine.

My set-up doesn't have a double-door system, but my ospreys have been slow in any escape attempts, so that lack has never been a problem. (I do have them for all other species).

When I show up daily to the mews, they often fly to the top and hover briefly, then circle once and land back on the perch. If I'm lucky. If not, they land on the floor, which creates handling issues.

Learning to Fly

As with any other bird, exposure to and teaching about hoods, anklets, and the glove are important. Make sure they reliably walk to the glove for food because this will lessen problems with skittishness and avoid the clumsiness with creances later.

Creances are enough trouble that I get them flying without using one. I do attach telemetry as soon as they appear physically capable of flying.

You watch them stretch and hop and practice for days. You hear the difference in sound when their flapping becomes effective and they hold themselves down to the ground or perch by gripping tightly. But you're still surprised when they actually take off.

When they fly off the first time, it'll be to a tree or roof nearby. They'll be reluctant to fly back down, so you'll be happy you trained them to come to your glove before the first flight.

I think the initial reluctance to come to the glove is due mostly to their lack of skill in landing. They're much quicker to come back to a tripod or nest perch, even if you're nearby.

Soon, they'll be practicing landings with a cautious eye towards wind direction and wing clearance. Some begin to practice diving just a few days after learning to fly. Sunny, breezy days make things easier for them.

Entering

Live fish in a barrel? Well, a shallow pool is a good start. They quickly learn some footwork here. For introducing them to prey, I used an assortment of frozen fish set on the bottom of the pool;

live fish hooked on a fishing line; floating dead fish; and live fish swimming in various size pools.

Once I moved into larger waters, I found that I could inject a thawed fish with a syringe full of air and throw it far out into the lake. It would reliably float back up for the osprey to catch.

To create a nearly free-swimming, submerged fish, I hooked a frisky bream on a short length of fishing line. I used a largish hook with a weighted head (the kind used for grub lures), dulled and with barb removed. This made it easier to pull out of the fish after the osprey had snagged it.

To keep this fish in a controlled position, I ran a six-foot line through the eye of a mushroom anchor sitting in one foot of water at the pond's edge. I held the other end, ready to release it as soon as the diving osprey pulled on it. I was concerned about potential entanglement or hooking issues, but this worked flawlessly many times.

To ensure a successful stoop from the boat, I pre-positioned sunken fish in the pond for him to discover. It was always a race with the turtles, which would quickly find my fish and drag them off.

It may be that none of this training is necessary. Ospreys seem to know the difference between a dead and live fish and approach dead ones with a floating, half-hearted dive. But if they see an active fish six inches below the surface, they'll fold in their wings, tuck their heads, and dive for it full-on—motions that appear to be instinctual as a whole package. Still, the footing introduction might be helpful, and the bird's coordination improves over time. Their instincts need practice to produce the impressive list of athletic skills necessary to catch a fish.

Hunting

My birds will sit patiently on a tall perch, looking for fish and diving, for up to two hours.

They'll hunt from elevated perches on my boat, T perches, or portable perches mounted to a tripod or even a golf cart! They'll fly over ponds and fish like wild birds do, but mine almost always prefer fishing from a perch.

To increase overall excitement, I typically encourage fish to come by feeding them; in the region where I live, this is the most productive method I've found.

My bream are fast, so multiple misses are the norm in my larger ponds.

Ospreys can catch very quick fish, however; I've seen them catch bluegill that were either stationary beneath the surface or rapidly striking at floating fish food.

With Ozzie, I also tried a tiny pond, about ten inches deep, with a few six- to seven-inch catfish in it. I didn't need to use food to lure those fish, as he could snag them while they slowly swam along the bottom of the pool.

I once took Ozzie to a friend's house to check out the catfish. The fish came to their feeding, as promised, and they were slow enough to be easy pickings, but they were huge. Ozzie head-bobbed away at these three-footers, but he wisely decided not to risk drowning trying to land one. (He wouldn't have drowned because I would have jumped in after him. I had pre-planned this unpleasantness and was already dreading the likely catfish finning. Catfish-finning pain is similar to falconry-footing pain—they both cause more suffering than the visible damage suggests.)

I see no reason to think ospreys are particular about the species of fish. The size is important, though, and there is a "too small" and a "too large." If it doesn't meet their criteria, they won't dive for it.

Suitable Prey for Ospreys

Like any other falconry, finding prey is an enormous part of the task. You may have to get creative. Fish, at least compared with other falconry prey, are easy to produce in quantity as well as to keep in a confined hunting area. I'm currently raising catfish because I feel certain that the osprey would make regular catches with these fish.

I suspect that the carp so prevalent in many areas of the country would also be reliable prey. Trout or appropriately sized, non-monstrous salmon in the spacious areas out west should work as well.

Commercial catfish operations or trout farms should be easy pickings, but if it gets too easy for the osprey, then I have some qualms about the "sport." Training is one matter, but if a pole fisherman would be hesitant to brag about the catch, so would I.

As is well known, however, fishermen aren't hesitant to brag about catching fish in stocked ponds or streams, so I consider this legitimate falconry.

Ultimately, my goal is to take the Grady White into the middle of the bay and let the osprey soar high until he crashes straight down onto a fourteen-inch Spanish Mackerel. He'll return to the perch set up for him on the boat. I'll secure him and his fish and head back to shore.

We're not there yet. Where we are now is fishing from tall shore perches or small boats or from the glove. The targets are fish coming to feed or lying on breeding beds or loitering along the bank. It's still an exciting challenge for me and the bird, but I would like to see them hunt from the air, stooping vertically after a hover.

This may never be. We rarely let our red-tails hunt for squirrels from a soar, but squirrel hawking is still fun, real falconry. So, even if my osprey isn't sailing above the seas, I am content.

Carrying

One fear about using ospreys is that, because they hunt over water, they can't stay where they catch their prey. It follows that they must catch something small enough they can fly with. (You might find a source of fish just the right size to prevent carrying, forcing the osprey to swim to shore, but that wouldn't be my first choice or theirs.)

Despite the numerous, attractive dead tree perches around my ponds, my birds have never landed high and away once they've caught a fish. They always choose to sit on perches in the yard, or on the lawn itself, or (rarely) on the grass across the pond.

In the latter instance, they have returned after eating, so far, either coming to the glove when called or just flying back to the perch. At first, I would boat across to retrieve them, but just waiting is less trouble.

The biggest inconvenience of calling them back after the catch is that they eat so slowly; you may have a thirty-minute wait. Mine never spook from me while eating and always allow me to approach when they are on a fish. They do mantle, however, and step or circle away from me if I try to get them on my glove.

Trading off doesn't present a big problem, but their slowness to release and lack of awareness (or over-concern) of their feet is an issue. I circumvent this by offering them a large piece of fish flesh, small enough to grasp with the beak, but too large to swallow. If I hold it directly to the beak, they'll grab it and release their catch. They reach up to hold and tear this new and ready-to-eat food, thus releasing their just-caught fish to me.

As they finish off this large tidbit, I towel clip the fish to my gauntlet then offer it to the bird from a couple of wingbeats away. It's almost always easier to get them to fly to you than step on to your glove from the ground.

I usually let them finish the fish they caught, partly on my glove, and partly in the mews. I make sure to feed them on the perches in the mews regularly, so it will continue to be an attractive place to them. They seem to prefer eating on pan perches rather than the pipe T perches.

Other Behavioral Notes and Concerns

Ozzie, my third bird, occasionally had what looked like panic attacks. He would mantle his fish and scream in an odd voice, spinning around clumsily, biting at the air. He bit me if I came close and sometimes bit at his own wing. These episodes lasted two to three minutes before he resumed eating.

Regarding the osprey "voice," they make a lot of noise unless focused. This language consists of variations on a theme. While their speech is limited to a series of short, repeated calls, I think several messages are decipherable: "I'm an uncomfortable young nestling"; "Here I am"; "I'm mad"; "I'm scared"; "I'm a little nervous"; "Feed me"; "Feed me now!" There are different intensities to several of these. They also make a brief chuckle sometimes which fits the improbable, "No one is listening so I might as well hunt for myself."

Many have noted the urge to migrate, and I've seen this myself. I think it would be prudent not to fly the birds during the fall. This should present no more problem to ospreys than putting up other species for the molt all summer.

By the Numbers

Nestling Numbers

For Ozzie, the youngest of my eyasses, an air temperature of around 90° F and contact surfaces up to 110° F seemed to be comfortable. He didn't pant or shiver at these levels, though he would shiver after eating lots of chilled fish.

The first day, he weighed 92 g and ate 46 g of fish. By that night, he weighed 120 g. The next morning, he was back down to 110 g. That day he ate 40 g and was up to 130 g that evening.

Every day, he gained about half the weight of the fish that he ate. The amount that he ate increased dramatically over time, and he grew visibly day to day.

Food

It will take about 45 full grown bream a month to feed one bird. These are not that easy to come by; catfish are easier. Around 20 eating-size catfish a month should work.

You can also buy whole frozen mullet. Each would last me two or three days, and the cost per pound is actually less than that of the quail or mice that other raptors eat.

Weights

I did some experimenting with weight on my second bird, Opie; here are the numbers.

Just before he began flying, his full crop weight was 1240 g. This was when he was eating all he would, with fish always available.

After that, I started feeding him one or two fish a day, filling his crop, but not to its max. If given a huge fish, he would slowly pack his whole crop tight, even packing his esophagus until you could actually see the fish. His highest weight ever was 1400 g. This was with one of these fully stuffed crops after several days of stuffing. At this weight, after emptying his crop, he was decidedly slow to come to me and clearly not hungry, but he did free fly and return!

The lowest weight was 894 g, and he was definitely weak at this level. I gave him two bream, and the next day he was at 1040 g. (My log from that day says that he caught bream number ten after "last millisecond correction!" I don't know exactly what I meant when I recorded that note, but I was clearly excited. I wish I kept better logs.)

Opie typically hovered around 950 to 1050 g. This is the weight at which he caught the vast majority of fish, and seemed healthy and happy. He made instant returns (for an osprey) to large tidbits and hunted when fish were around. (Ospreys only launch vigorously for live prey.) If there were no fish in sight, he turned towards me and begged.

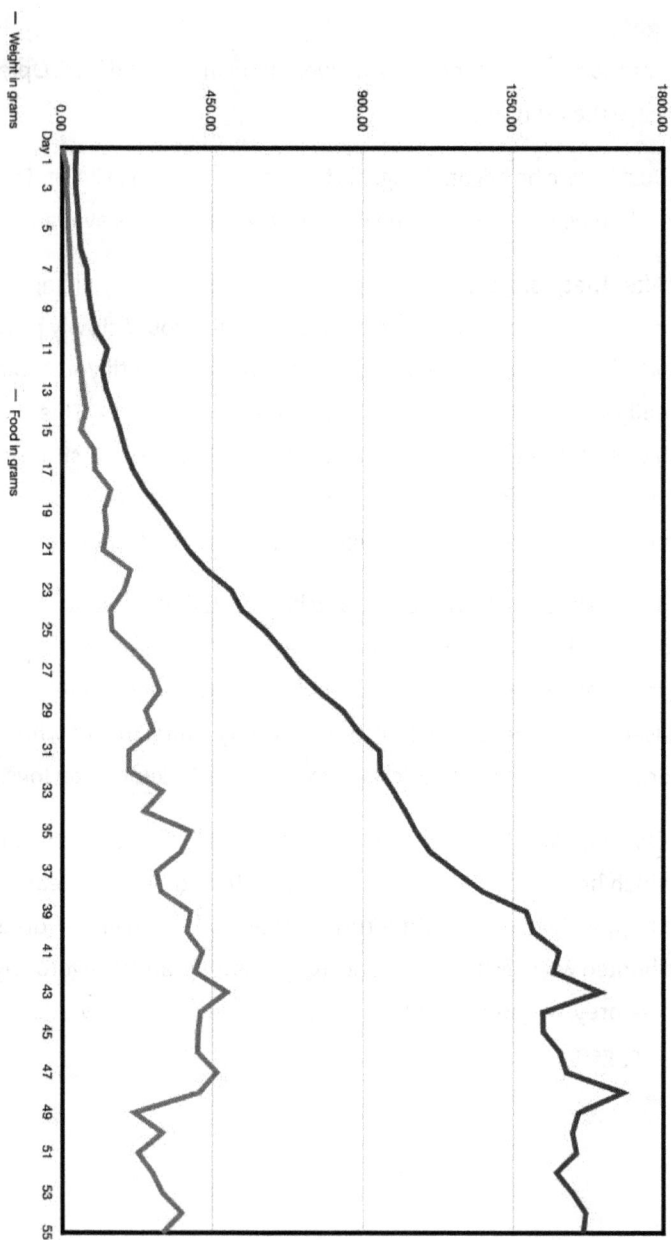

Osprey Nestling Growth

— Weight in grams — Food in grams

SECTION 3:

Handling

Some of the information is this section has already been mentioned in other areas, but I wanted to paint a good picture of what
it's like to work with an osprey. Ospreys are a little different in their
needs; getting them on scales, carrying them around, and predict-
ing their actions is not as simple as it is for other falconry birds.

I would be shocked if ospreys were truly "stupid," but the disconnect between catching prey and eating, coupled with their
slow-motion anxiety, is probably what gives this reputation. They
are different and frustrating if one expects them to behave like a
redtail. Like owls, they have a personality distinct from other raptors.

Difficulties in Handling

The first factor to consider is their "slow anxiety." For instance,
when an osprey is looking at your glove and head bobbing, he will
come to you—it will just be a minute.

Like departing in a huge airliner, there are procedures to follow,
and there will be a more than slight delay. They have to make sure
they have not already grasped a fish, that an eagle is not after them,
and that the wind conditions are OK for the flight.

After working with them, I don't think this pause indicates a too-heavy condition, as it would with a redtail. Therefore, I do not think it is wise to drop weight in trying to get an instant response. If they're too slow, using very large tidbits can speed the response, but trying repeated flights to small tidbits doesn't lead to increased speed as they can lose interest, especially on longer flights.

Secondly, they are not quick on their feet. The talons are designed for grabbing and holding onto fish, for perching, and for feeding. Their legs, as well, are built for perching and grabbing fish, but not for leaping from perches or hopping onto gloves.

If you think about it, it makes sense that ospreys wouldn't be good at jumping. Jumping would not be helpful in a water takeoff with osprey-style feet. This reluctance or even inability to hop accounts for many handling oddities.

One last thing worth mentioning is that these birds seem to hold grudges. I have seen reluctance to return after I annoyed them with messing about with something new, like anklets or hooding. Several hours after a disagreement, however, they seem to re-evaluate you as a safe partner.

Perch Behavior

It's a fairly standard procedure to pick an osprey up off a T perch. Put your glove under his chest, sometimes touching him, and he will step up. The difference is that he will never just hop; he will step laboriously or even fully deploy his wings and use them to assist in the step up.

On the other hand, they're very difficult to pick up from a spacious perch or from the ground. You can't simply restrain them with jesses and expect them to hop. (They would pull away backwards, risking the tail.)

Putting a glove to their chest when they are on the ground is frequently unsuccessful. They may just walk away. More commonly, they will step up with one foot on the glove but not follow this by stepping with the second foot. Instead, they will step back off your glove and circle counterclockwise to avoid the falconer who is looming over them.

My pan perches are more spacious than a T perch, and, therefore, give the osprey more opportunity to shy away. When I offer the glove to my current bird, he just spins away on the perch. If I circle around the perch with him, he will eventually stop avoiding me and step up after about three circuits in parallel. I just have to be careful to give him room for his wings.

I have also tried pushing the bird sideways back on to my glove as they veered away. This works but is clearly inelegant. One bird would habitually peck my thumb as he stepped up with his right leg. This was good, because this pecking would usually lead to him stepping fully up with his left one also, to place his talon right next to his beak as in an eating maneuver.

Once, I tried to pick up a hooded bird in the mews. He stepped up well enough, but flapped vigorously, beating me about the face as he ascended my arm to my upper back. (The blinded-big-bird-on-the-back situation was solved by the intervention of my capable son. It would have been tricky and more painful without him.)

Sometimes, as you try to get them onto the glove, they hop off the perch onto the floor. A crude fix is to pick them up gently and place them back on the perch, then start over. However, it seems best to call them to your glove with a tidbit if they are on the floor or ground. Though they are sometimes reluctant to fly any significant distance just for a tidbit, they are reliable when close enough to see that it's fish flesh.

They are a little slow to be backed onto a scale perch for weighing, but it is sometimes doable as long as they have room to spread wings. It is far easier to position the scale in front of them. I often pick the bird up and place it on the scale, but I hesitate to recommend this since it seems so confrontational.

Hooding

Getting a hood on them is not too bad. Ozzie, bird three, was easier than any bird I've had, osprey or otherwise. My current bird, however, has been reluctant, vigorously using all his osprey ducking and dodging skills. I exposed him very early to the hood, but otherwise took no great pains, since I expected the ease of the prior bird. It seemed to be going well until he discovered how supple his neck was.

Because I am trying harder to use anklets and jesses on this current bird, I am receiving increasingly hostile pecks. Having tired of this, I mostly do my hooding in the safety of the mews, while adding telemetry or jesses. Doing so relieves all of the pecking.

It turns out that the clumsiness of ospreys is handy when it comes time for hooding. As he tries to circle away on the perch or floor, ducking and dodging all the while, I can use my left hand to block his spin and stabilize his head so hooding is easy. This doesn't seem to bother him too much; a less clumsy redtail would likely have footed me badly.

I haven't tried using the normal method of hooding while the bird is already on the fist, though I could easily do so with Ozzie. This particular bird has a tendency to fall off perches backwards when avoiding his hood. And, aside from that, I am resolved to maintain my fist as a happy place for him; so I have avoided associating any hood animosity with the glove.

Transportation

The osprey's wide-spreading-wing reaction has given me bad luck when trying to back them into a normal giant hood, the typical box with a door in the front.

Of course, a giant hood is helpful to protect your bird and wing feathers in a vehicle, as well as to protect your vehicle from the widely slung, particularly smelly and staining, mutes. I did not want to give up using one, but I did quickly learn that the traditional design would not work.

With the traditional boxes, ospreys' clumsiness when stepping back and their need to spread their wings made getting them safely in or out of the box problematic. Not to mention, they rarely stay quiet and calm; their tail feathers are at great risk while they flail in close quarters.

As my first attempt at an alternative, I tried a plastic dog crate. *Maybe an open view will help calm him*, I thought. Wrong. He had soon jumped up and grabbed the wire front, snapping off the tips of some tail feathers as he hung from the door. Anything but calm.

At last, I developed the giant hood detailed in the "Equipment" appendix. Some towels on the floor of the box, arranged around the central perch, will mostly collect the mutes as they run down the interior sides. Thus far, there has been no feather soiling, but when traveling I carry a water spray bottle for cleanup in case.

Eventually, I'll replace this makeshift design with something more aesthetically pleasing, though it will probably be more expensive, heavier, and harder to clean; I'm in no rush.

On the Fist

Ospreys do not handle bating from the glove well. They regain the fist like a red-tailed hawk on its very first bate; that is, they don't regain without lots of help. Unlike the redtail, the osprey's tail is just waiting to be broken.

On the other hand, they don't bate much. They also give some warning — leaning away from you and shifting weight. This allows prevention by distraction; if you point to the glove or tidbit, they will typically decide to stay a little longer.

When the bird is on the fist, you have to be careful walking through doors. Don't be surprised by any sudden flapping of the long wings, and be mindful of the brittle feather tips. If you stumble a little, they will also. If they show signs of instability, you should pause until they are in a better position.

Tethers, Leathers, and Telemetry

I placed my last bird on a flat carpet with a centrally located swivel and a one-inch high felt board perch. He tolerated being tethered to this setup well, hooded or not. This should work with a large enough table also.

The typical bow or ring or block perches will work, but you have to have a really long leash to avoid tail issues. I would not leave one unsupervised in this condition.

Overall, I haven't tried hard with tethering, because I hunt in my backyard and have the combination mews/weathering pen. There's little need for it in my situation.

As far as leather goes, my current bird is handling normal anklets, jesses, and swivels. When fishing, I have him in anklets only, then secure him to my glove with lobster clips. Otherwise, I only secure him to large flat surfaces such as the center of a table perch or an extremely low block perch (around four inches) or a pan perch low to the ground.

I have been able to attach telemetry to his anklet without difficulty as long as he is hooded. The feisty pecking is too much if he is not hooded, and I still occasionally get a mild peck even then. The best news is that after several unintentional provocations, there has been no hint of footing!

Conclusion

Is the Bird Right for You?

Falconers have a wide variety of birds to work with. Why should you even consider using a bird as difficult as an osprey? Here are my thoughts on the matter.

First, for the skeptics: Osprey fishing is successful and exciting falconry. I love these birds up close. They have character, and they're gorgeous in flight. I see plenty of stoops—some, dramatic. I see enough catches not to feel thwarted. The prey may be cold-blooded little fish and not birds or mammals, but the stoops and soars are magnificent and just as exciting as other falconry experiences.

Falconry with ospreys opens up new potential. With ample bodies of water around, hunting grounds are easy to come by. I can also fish with them year-round. (Though, note that I obtained a fishing license. I don't think any law regulates fishing with an osprey, but public bodies of water may present an issue.)

Ospreys are relatively safe to handle. Despite the dangerous-looking talons, ospreys are less likely to seriously injure you than other common falconry birds. I get harmlessly (but a little painfully) pecked, but never footed. My eyes seem safe—a nice change from my Cooper's hawks. Carrying, handling, and husbandry have issues,

but not insurmountable ones. The mistakes a falconer makes with an osprey aren't usually hazardous.

In the Eastern U.S., osprey eyasses are more readily and safely available than other wild species. Nests are widespread, and you don't have to be a mountaineer or climbing arborist to reach them.

Of course, I'm not suggesting doing anything that would harm the osprey population; worldwide availability will vary greatly. It's possible, even likely, that those of you in other places have no ethical access to a bird.

As something of an aside, I hope to see more ospreys in the bird display business. They should be great ambassadors for our waterways. I can't be the only person who fell in love with these birds the first time I saw a picture! That love for an individual species is frequently the basis for a broader passion for improving the environment.

I can envision them in the typical raptor show; they would be suitable for it, but you may need several birds for multiple shows. They should reliably fly to tidbits on nice big perches but may be hesitant. Handlers could safely display them on a large table perch. A dramatic fishing display could be set up with an elevated mews over a small, heavily stocked pond.

Are You Right for the Bird?

That said, I don't recommend ospreys for beginners, if only because of the lack of resources and widespread experience. Although I'm sure some must be around, I know of no other falconers currently using ospreys. And you can find volumes of information and help on other birds.

Aside from that, ospreys possess many quirks that make them unsuitable for beginners. Traditional birds offer more predictable behavior and the likelihood of success. It's helpful to gain experience judging what annoys or frightens other raptors before tackling an osprey.

Furthermore, ospreys are big, and their feathers are fragile. It's best to have a feel for how raptors move before handling them.

But after success with other birds, typically as a late General or Master Falconer, anyone who loves these birds should give ospreys a try. It will take patience, but no more than when handling a passage Cooper's hawk.

Having a suitable situation is another important factor. To duplicate my circumstances, you'll need an area of land, with a mews placed next to hunting ponds. My ponds are only partially lined with trees, so I can access all sides, and the birds can fly for hundreds of yards in all directions.

These trained birds seem to be territorial, and specifics of my location may have been critical to my success, although I doubt this. Other situations are likely to work, as well. I can imagine an osprey and falconer operating happily from a mews built on a boat on a large lake.

I'd honestly be too lazy to hunt with an osprey if I didn't live next to water, but you don't need a proper lake or ocean. Even a small pond would be fun for you and a sufficient workout for the bird. Multiple dives and water launches are vigorous exercise and don't require huge amounts of space. A pond more heavily surrounded by trees (except for the landing area) may even help prevent any carrying.

I've found the availability of live, largish fish to be essential to my methods, but a creative type might get around this.

Take into consideration that ospreys can be annoying. Mine have screamed a lot. They're ungainly on the ground and in tight quarters. When in training, the slow eating, with the long hesitancy before beginning and the frequent pauses throughout, can test one's patience. They are slow to do whatever you want them to do.

But despite all this, I hope other bird lovers will give it a try and fine tune the handling. Then we can increasingly enjoy these birds, and the birds will enjoy themselves.

The End

As you reach the end of my osprey experiences (so far), I hope you will agree with me: Osprey falconry is real falconry.

And even if it's not—by someone else's stringent definition—then I respond that it's fun. (And, in the US, you need a falconry license to do it. Interpret that as you will.)

If you choose to follow in my footsteps, please remember these are early experiments. The process should improve over time. You can search many resources online for help with husbandry for rehabbers, and I'd suggest that any falconer considering ospreys check these out.

I have more ideas and more plans, but for now, this is it. My osprey journey continues. Now that this book is finished, we'll head down to the pond. It's a sunny day for soaring and splashing, and maybe we'll catch a big one!

Appendix I: Equipment

The Portable Nest

This design is durable, portable, and easy for the bird to recognize. They'll return to it in preference to anything else, unless it's placed somewhere really scary. It's probably even more reliable for returns when used in the mews as the primary perch also, but I prefer the perch I'll detail later for feather protection reasons.

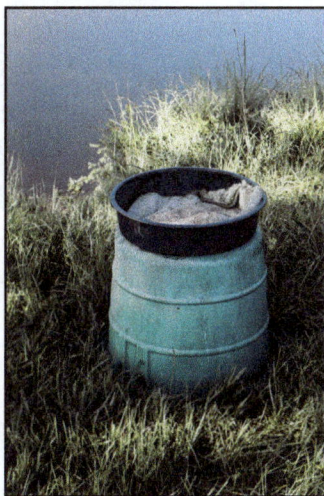

For this perch, I got a feed pan (I have lots of these, as I use to have sheep) and mounted it right side up to the bottom of a bigger, deep watering tub which is situated upside down. I bolted it on securely. You can fill it with pine-straw, towels, or carpeting; each has its pros and cons.

The edge of the pan needs to be smooth, since tailfeathers will regularly brush against it.

If the padding is too skimpy, they can push the back of their tails against the sides of the pan. This is why I also use completely flat perches (like the tripod perch) once they're capable of avoiding fall injuries.

The Tripod Perch

This perch is great for uneven surfaces and fishing on the banks of ponds. I use a surveyor's transit tripod as the base. These are very sturdy, easily adjustable, and light. I drill some holes in the tripod top, attach a board, then screw an upside-down plastic feed pan to the board and cover it with artificial turf.

The Giant Hood

It's not chic, but it's quick. I found a 30-gallon plastic tub big enough for him to clear when perched longwise, but not quite large enough for him to rotate around in without touching his tail. I melted four vent holes in the ends and a larger hole in the top that doubled as a handle. Since the bird would also be hooded inside, the main function was to contain the bird and his mutes. The plastic was not opaque, but since he was hooded, providing darkness as in a normal hawk box was less of a priority.

You need a "helper perch" to get the bird in; for this, I got a flat, one-inch thick, six-inch wide board and wrapped it with artificial turf.

Using this giant hood requires several steps.

First, hood the osprey. Prepare your space by having the top of the plastic tub nearby, upside-down.

Next, offer the board "helper perch" for the osprey to step up to by holding it to his breast.

When the bird is safely on the artificial turf, place the helper perch in position on the upside-down top.

Now, you can carefully lower the body of the tub over the bird.

I drilled little holes in the corners of the assembled top and bottom so I could fasten them together more securely, not relying on the built-in catch. Careful handing is necessary, but the ospreys predictably stand on the turf and avoid the adjacent exposed board.

The helper perch board, or a similar object, also comes in handy when the osprey is in a position to back onto a perch. This is a little tricky for them, so placing the osprey on this super portable perch allows you to convert a stepping-back scenario into the much easier stepping-forward situation.

The Tall Hunting Perch

A pole of 1.5" PVC pipe with an upside-down feed pan attached to the top makes a light and weather-worthy perch.

I cover the top with artificial turf or indoor/outdoor carpet, using hot glue. This has held up well and is quick to put together. Lacing it down with zipties and drilled holes works, as well, but is more labor. I use standardized colors for the carpet and pan across all my perches to possibly help with recognition and return.

To place this perch as a hunting spot pondside, I drive a large metal stake into the ground and slide the PVC pipe over it. These stakes are available in the concrete supply areas of big-box home supply stores.

When landing, the birds frequently swoop upwards at the last second and grab the edge of the perch. They will use the carpeting extending to the edge as a point of purchase, almost pulling themselves up as opposed to floating downwards to it. They give a little when the osprey lands, swaying, but that doesn't seem to affect the bird.

I have a simple hole-in-a-board box mount that allows this perch to be clamped to vehicles. I also have a specially shaped board with a large hole drilled into it to affix the perch to the bow of a boat.

The PVC pipe can be sectioned and made more portable using inline connectors (of course, no glue!).

I have also used tall PVC T perches (a pipe covered with carpet or artificial turf). These are more handy than flat pan perches in certain situations (such as lowering the bird to the ground while it can still keep a grip), but the birds sometimes struggle to simultaneously hold themselves and the fish on them while eating.

Towel Clips

These surgical tools, available cheaply online, are essential for gripping both fish tidbits and caught prey. Fish are extremely slippery, and ospreys tug hard with their beaks while eating and while trying to leave. A towel clip is an easy way to grab hold onto the fish, even without much room to move under a man-tling, pecking bird.

Grasping the body just ahead of the tail is good because the osprey prefers to eat the head first, but the fish can be torn loose from this position. Clipping the tool through the fish lip is more secure, but more of a problem to the feeding osprey. You may need to go back and forth between the two.

I augment the tool by tying a lanyard through one of the handle loops and placing a French clip on the other end. This allows for securing the fish to the glove. With this, I can also secure the fish to the perch as a means of letting the osprey eat with less chance of carrying.

Leatherworks

A Steve Tait size 24 hood fit three of my birds perfectly.

The typical anklet/jesse would likely be fine, but I prefer legs bare or just with anklets. If just using anklets, I secure them to the glove or perch with dog leash lobster clips—the kind with symmetrically closing jaws; I sometimes have to grind them a little smaller to fit smoothly through the anklet grommets.

I occasionally use easily removable (but not very secure) jesses and anklets on supervised birds.

It's possible bells would work, but you may have to improve their water draining capabilities. I also think they would produce too much water drag, so I haven't tried them.

Telemetry

Telemetry is always a great idea on a bird prone to carry. I under-utilized it initially due to fears of malfunction due to all the dunking.

Sometimes, the birds also mistake the leg-mounted transmitter as a catch and will grasp the device, circling around in their typical post-catch manner before landing. It then takes them a few minutes to decide it's inedible before they will consider hunting again or returning to you.

My current bird, just starting to dive, usually sports a leg mount that has been dunked dozens of times. I initially sealed it with jesse grease which lasted about a week. After drying out the drowned transmitter, it began working again. I then sealed it with some tough paint, and that has held up over a month.

My first foray to big water will include at least a leg mount. I'll seal the transmitter with some silicon.

A backpack mounted transmitter might work since the mount would be protected from most water forces in a dive, but it's rarely a good idea to mix water and ropes. (Scuba divers always carry knives for a reason.)

A tail mount would possibly damage feathers during a dive. Some takeoffs necessitate vigorous downward thrusting of the tail; this might also be a problem for the tail mount.

Appendix II: Interesting Little Falconry Episodes

Nothing is fictionalized or exaggerated. Even the names are real.

Blind Redtail

Several years ago, my wife and I drove through the city searching for a red-tailed hawk. We spotted one in a park, perched on a streetlamp. With a curious audience watching, I set a noose-covered trap under the light and waited. After a moment, the bird flew down and attached to the trap. I rushed over, and, to simplify, I secured his feet and put him in a box. A smooth capture.

It wasn't until we got him home that I noticed the bird's right eye had an opaque appearance. That was concerning, but I thought he was worth a try, even with the one bad eye. I began training him to sit on my glove.

The RT manned without issue, but whenever I approached him from the right, he startled.

In the end, I decided he wouldn't make a good hunting hawk because I could lose him too easily. If the bird perched in a tree at some distance, and I was standing on his right side, he might never see me.

We returned him to the riverside park where we'd found him. But before we left, I tossed a quail out for him. He parachuted down, accepted this parting gift, and then settled onto a large oak branch to eat.

Two years later, we were searching for hawks in the city once again. This time, we glimpsed one on a metal tower. We set out a trap on the sidewalk, drove forward a few yards, and waited. The bird swooped down, not approaching directly, but oddly curving counterclockwise as he descended. When his feet caught in the trap nooses, we hurried over to grab him and discovered he was the same blind hawk I had manned! His curving approach allowed him see with his one good eye. We let him loose, and he flew away. No doubt, he's still hunting over his urban territory near the river.

Sora the Redtail

Sora was a small redtail I caught as a passage bird. He was a natural squirrel bird and extremely athletic. He was also more of a hazard to our farm animals than my other raptors have been.

We used to have a small flock of wandering peacocks. They refused to stay home, despite having unlimited food and sixty acres and began wandering about, wearing out welcomes. At some point, the neighbors two miles away notified animal control, and the birds were put on probation.

The animal control officer did some surveillance and identifed the ringleader—a gorgeous Java Green Peafowl. After repeated trespassing incidents, we got rid of the unrepentant birds peacefully, and deposited them at a friend's farm. (He wanted them, mistakenly confident that 200 acres would be plenty).

But back to Sora. Before we were rid of the peacock flock, Sora and I were squirrel-hawking a few hundred yards from home. He was high in the trees when he became fixated on something and took off in a long stoop. I was a little annoyed that he was backtracking, but I still assumed a squirrel was his target.

I grew more annoyed when I saw that he was headed out of the woods. This was unlikely a squirrel and quite possibly a distracting wild redtail.

I was, well, apprehensive when I realized he was crossing back over the pond towards the house where cats and dogs milled about outside. I couldn't imagine whatever other mischief the bird might get up to.

The peacocks erupted in squawking. A fight was under way!

I started my 800-yard dash. I didn't know what to expect, but I did have a clue.

This hawk had already attacked one of our large Muscovy ducks. Afterwards, the flock had banded together to ward him off, but he generally ignored them. One day, a single, lonely drake was dabbling in the mud with his head down and his neck outstretched—too tempting. Sora dove into temptation from a tree, bound to the fowl's neck, and by the time I had finished my one hundred-yard dash, it was dead.

Well, as the above duck tale would suggest, when I reached the yard, winded after my long run, Sora was also winded while holding a grown peacock in a Full Nelson death grip.

My wife wasn't amused when informed.

Pierre the Peregrine

Pierre was a scrappy little male peregrine shipped south to me from New York. I flew him on farm-raised quail and tried unsuccessfully to fly him on crows. (He did bind to a crow, but the rest of the murder mobbed him and chased him from it.)

On his very first flight, this falcon fled an attacking red-shouldered hawk from the top of my chimney. The wild hawk was gaining on him initially, but Pierre quickly began pulling away. On this, his first flight, he realized he was master of the local skies, and thereafter, he acted like it. He would chase off any vulture or hawk that came within eyesight; he patrolled overhead, circling, until I stirred up a quail or an interloper appeared. Pierre and I had a good five years.

He hurt me a few times over those years, but he rarely meant to. Once, while he was stooping to a swung lure, going about seventy, he plowed into my side. Needless to say, this knocked the breath out of me, and knocked him briefly loopy. I was surprised the impact didn't kill him.

Another time, I was walking along a tree line scaring up quail. One flew away from Pierre, who was waiting only a couple hundred feet up. As the quail flushed, I stepped into a small gap where I could follow the action.

This, unfortunately, happened to be the same gap Pierre had chosen for his tail chase, and he whacked into the side of my head. I temporarily lost my sunglasses, hat, and possibly some memories. Pierre hit the ground, sort of bounced, and took off again in pursuit!

On another occasion, he was perched on the chimney, scanning for any interlopers about the farm, when a wild pigeon landed on the opposite end of the roof. Within a second, Pierre turned his head towards the pigeon who instantly noticed this and bolted.

The pigeon crossed the lake with Pierre pumping hard in pursuit and gaining. The pigeon quickly calculated this situation and dove into a bush on the other side of the lake. Pierre was accustomed to ending chases for quail in pretty thick cover, so the pigeon's cleverness was to no avail.

After a quick canoe trip, I found a breathless Pierre, wings askance in the bush, plucking away at his dead catch.

My saddest Pierre story begins with him high overhead. Just as I pulled out my lure, he plummeted in attack on something across the farm. One of the quail I had about, I assumed. He disappeared behind a tree at the last moment, and I heard a squawk, one I'd never heard before. It sounded vaguely like Pierre. This gave me a sense of foreboding.

I was hoping to see Pierre winging back up above the trees, but I saw nothing.

After a long, telemetry-guided hike, I stirred up a juvenile red-tail that only flew when I came within fifty feet of him. After that unusual occurence, I was prepared: I found Pierre intact, but dead, lying next to a headless squirrel.

I wasn't there to see it, but I suspect he had spotted the feeding redtail and tried to steal the squirrel. This fearless little bird had flown low in too much cover, where his speed wasn't so helpful.

Reluctant Redtail

One redtail refused to come back to me for a week, although she was happy to use me as a prey flusher for several of those days.

It started with a very reluctant return, a bungled attempt at tethering on the glove, followed by increasingly desperate measures (including a rejected bal-chatri hamster). She rewarded these efforts by flying off to roost that evening.

The next morning, I could hear her cheery bells a few hundred yards from the house. She let me get close and she followed very well, but she always stayed in the trees and wouldn't return to fist or lure. We hunted together every morning for a week, but not successfully.

I finally got her back in hand using a frozen squirrel carcass covered in nooses. Upon retrieval, she acted like nothing had happened. Fifty grams less weight and smoother handling was all she needed.

Head-Squeezing Incident

Earlier, I mentioned using the "head-squeezing" technique on a red-tailed hawk in an unsuccessful attempt to save Opie. Although this technique didn't work on the redtail bound to my osprey, it worked for me once. This maneuver is frequently alluded to in falconry books, but I haven't read reports of it in action. I have a report to make.

My very first bird, a female redtail, was calmly sitting on my glove, a little bit higher on the arm than I like. She decided to take another step and placed her foot on my bare skin, her talons encircling my biceps tendon. I couldn't coax her to move, and all my increased attention made her squeeze harder.

I tried to trade her off to perches, but she was, for some reason, content where she was. As my blood seeped around her talons, I walked outside to see if she would be interested in flying off.

She wasn't. My tiring arm was beginning to quiver, which made her increase the grip and depth of penetration. Soon, my "man's best friend" ambled over to pick up any dropped tidbits. His furry presence further endangered my future arm function and increased my present pain.

As I ran out of options, I decided to employ the "Head Squeeze" I'd read about somewhere. I grabbed her entire head and squeezed gently. She quickly released me, and I was physically relieved but afraid she would desert me forever after my "assault." She flew away from my blood dripping arm and landed on a tree limb nearby. I was fully relieved when she returned promptly to a tidbit as if nothing had happened.

Alex the Barn Owl

Alex got lots of attention. All the visitors loved him and he posed with them for photographs. He got lots of "oohs and ahs" over these. It was just his looks, because his personality was not so fetching. Feisty, moody and selfish with food, he hissed dissatisfaction with most of what humans did.

I flew him around the farm at twilight or sometimes in pitch black dark. I adorned him with flashing balloon lights for night flights, but I didn't use telemetry because he was such a homebody. He frequently flew back into his mews after a few bites. He always hissed his location and was very quick to come to any hint of food. His approach was eerily quiet and sometimes a little frightening when he appeared abruptly in the dark. I sorely missed him when he flew away.

One twilight hunt, he left suddenly. He took off on one of his usual flightpaths, but he veered sharply and disappeared around the back of the barn. He did not reappear as expected at the other end. After a few moments, I went behind the barn in search, but he was nowhere to be seen.

Of course, I spent hours calling and whistling while walking over the whole farm. I couldn't find him. I thought it was most likely that a Cooper's hawk had gotten him. He was gone for good.

Some months later, the sight of some droppings from a large bird streaking down his favorite corner of the garage roof made me think of him, and added a little to my sadness. Around that same time, I coincidently noted the evidence of a large bird "disrespecting" our car with a dropping.

Neither of these occurrences seemed remarkable until I was startled by Alex flying out of the garage one morning as I was leaving the house for work! It had been months, and I was shocked to see him and happy he was alive. I tried to attract him, but he flew away. He looked me in the eye, but he was in no mood to hang around. He acted as if I had disturbed his rest. It was light by now and time for him to be sleeping. It was not time for me to sleep, however, and my work time was inflexible, so I could not make any immediate attempts to retrieve him. I spent all day at work making plans and hoping.

As soon as I got home after my shift, I began repairing my Swedish goshawk trap. I was hammering away, making a racket in the driveway. My son walked up behind me and with nonchalance said, "Alex is in the tree." Sure enough, Alex was in a tree fifty feet behind me, watching me work on his trap!

I quickly got my glove and some food and tried to attract him. He eyed me, but was not interested in returning, keeping himself aloof in high branches. He acted a little skittish (as you would expect after all this time) and when I got closer, he retreated one tree over. It was still an hour before sunset.

I quickly set up a bal-chatri trap with a gerbil and placed this under him. He looked and looked and leaned towards it, but wouldn't go for it. I also tried his lure with no success.

While I was trying out my options, a cicada began calling on a limb nearby him. The buzz of the bug abruptly stuttered, then silenced as Alex pounced on it for a snack.

He ignored all my increasingly frantic trapping attempts for an hour. The sun set and twilight began. In the dimmer light, in a pleasant surprise, Alex just flew down to my glove for a tidbit as if he had merely been gone for his daily flight! My heart skipped as I fumbled securing him, and he flew up to the garage roof. He quickly returned for another tidbit, and this time I was more determined and clipped him to my glove. He sat and ate up, behaving no differently than the day before he flew away.

He weighed about fifty grams more than when he left. When he disappeared, I suppose he must have flown around the barn and caught something himself, instead of getting caught by something as I feared. He must have found plenty of food. A couple of feathers were out of place, but otherwise he seemed fine. He didn't act offended to be returned to the mews.

Of course, those big droppings on the roof and car were clear hints that he was around (hints I missed.) He probably was visiting each night. I just never made the connection.

Now wiser, I decided to slow him down slightly with telemetry. A leg mount only annoyed him slightly and wasn't a noticeable problem in the thick weeds (my real reason for not using telemetry before.) He was more interested in hunting after his return.

I still fly this barn owl as a falconry bird. We catch rats. Twelve, at last count. That doesn't include the unconfirmed kills. While I don't necessarily believe a body count is the best measure of falconry success, some people do. Still, I'd like to explain that I really think we've caught more than twelve.

If you're wondering how I can have "unconfirmed" kills, let me describe how the barn owl hunts. He slowly floats around the farm about ten feet above the rough pastures that house our local rodent population. Every few minutes or so, he wheels over and plummets feet-first, straight to the ground with his wings and face held upwards to the sky. He disappears into the grass, briars, or weeds. In less than a second, he thrusts his beak down to his talons, trying to snap up the head of the mouse, vole, or rat.

Lots of times, he bounces back into the air. This means a miss. If he tarries more than a minute, there's a good chance he's caught something.

The first rat he caught was a big one. He was clearly excited when he popped up out of the tall grass. He flew about twenty-five yards, laboring under the weight of the rat, before landing again. I approached him and picked him up, together with his prize. He held the rat firmly in his beak, but it was too large for him to swallow whole, in his usual fashion.

On other occasions, I either retrieved him while he was trying to eat a rat too big to swallow in one gulp, or I watched him carry it (bad bird) and slowly eat it elsewhere. (And afterwards, the pig would return for a tidbit!)

There were dozens of other times it's likely he caught smaller prey. This little bird can swallow a whole grown mouse in a few seconds, with no trace left. So, when he disappeared in the grass longer than usual, gained more weight than he should have from tidbits, or returned with bloody talons, he probably killed something. It was impossible to know for sure, of course, since he was buried in grass maybe fifty yards away. Thus, my "assumed kills."

He is not a peregrine, but I love this little bird. He gets to fly and hunt regularly. He flies hundreds of yards during each hunt and returns at once when I call (except in definite or assumed kill situations).

We have undeniably taken prey, according to the dictionary definition of falconry. He's not merely a pet.

In my mind, I'm having loads of fun with a challenging bird. It's falconry. It's successful. It's just varied. The sport that includes car hawking kestrels and peregrines and the tricky passage Cooper's surely has room for the occasional owl.

Appendix III:
The Story of Neptune

"Neptune — Adventures with an Osprey"

Originally published by and reprinted with kind permission of
Wild und Hund 70(23):559-560, 1968.70

By Hugo Richter

Translated from the German by Daniel McLendon

In the thirties, shortly before my university entrance exams, my grandfather was an active forester in a Thuringian hunting district. We had a few fishponds belonging to the forestry service that teemed with carp. Ospreys lived there as nesting birds and resident birds. An old book I once read mentioned that in earlier times these raptors had been trained to hunt fish. But I could find no other details as to how they were trained.

By chance I observed one of the ospreys catching its prey. The bird miscalculated and landed with the fish in a large, exposed fish trap, where neither could get free. I rushed forward with my fishing net and pulled them from their prison. The fish was already dead, while the osprey tried but failed to extricate itself. I brought him to the house and let him settle down in an empty goat pen. He immediately perched on the trough and sat there anxiously.

In order to tame him, or, as the falconers say, to man him, I followed R. Waller's detailed prescriptions with regard to wild-caught hawks or falcons. The osprey received a full crop of fish daily from the pond that I caught live for him. He flapped around his perch and eyed the wriggling fish, but dared come no closer. I stood still as a statue and began to quietly speak to him. Although I remained near him for half-an-hour, he did not take the fish. On the next day I tried again. It may have simply been hunger, but in any case, he hastily took the fish from my hand and immediately sprang back to his perch, where he devoured it.

In the meantime I built a mews with the help of my grandfather, who listened with a smile as I explained my intention to train the osprey and opined that I would make a fool of myself, but let me proceed all the same. My grandfather also thought I should put a hood on the osprey, but I ignored this, pointing out that he wore no cap in the wild. Besides, there were trained hawks and eagles that were not hooded. Ospreys, I reasoned, as pure fish-specialists could hardly be distracted or unsettled by other wild creatures. This insight proved true. Neptune, as I christened him, comported himself as a noble eagle, whom nothing could disturb from his quiet, except fish.

So, Neptune was not hooded. By my care and good nourishment, the osprey grew sleek and quite impressive. I weighed him daily, and his weight remained constantly near 1.5 to 1.8 kgs. It should be pointed out that this weight and the good condition of the feathers are necessary for successful hunting.

First, I put ordinary hawk jesses on Neptune and during the day I put him on a perch in the clearing before the goat pen. These raptors' peculiar mode of hunting made some thinking about the jesses necessary. Putting contraptions on their feet is a nuisance since they always dive feet-first. One also shouldn't put bells on an osprey. These only fill up with water, making them useless.

After many attempts to discover jesses that could be loosened with one pull, I gave up. Anyway, Neptune had become so tame that he would stand on my fist without jesses and no longer showed any inclination to escape. He flew freely among the trees and followed the way to the pond, where he waited for me. It was similarly difficult accustoming him to falcon bird lures. He showed no interest whatsoever in these lures that occupied the hawks and falcons in my grandfather's estate. He just plucked little tidbits off the lures and considered this sufficient. But I needed to teach him to hand over his prey to his human hunting-companion, while he could fill his crop with the lure's tidbits. He also refused a fish lure that I carefully constructed from a two-summer carp. He just plucked off pieces of fish and took refuge in the next willow tree or simply hopped on my fist.

Then it occurred to me that the osprey could not react to anything that crawled on the ground or flew in the air, because his prey is in the water. Like release pigeons for hawks or falcons, I stocked a barrel with more two-summer carp and provided it with a slider that was large enough that the fish could shoot out into the pond-water. After some practice I got the hang of it, and the fish participated with no little excitement.

Now it got serious. I set up the barrel with the release-hole directly over the water. It was easy to open with a pulley. With Neptune on my fist, I placed myself ten meters from the barrel. I gave my cousin, who was helping, a signal. The feeder flew up, and with a jet of water, the first carp shot out and splashed into the water. Neptune jerked to attention and peered intently at the barrel, from which the second fish was already darting. He began to dance, and as the third fish left the barrel for freedom, Neptune plunged from my fist, made a short turn and plunged talons-foremost in the water, which sprayed up and coated bird and fish alike. After about two seconds, he reemerged, pumped hard with his wings, and carried off the stricken fish, which had already succumbed to his knife-like talons.

Because of the received wisdom that ospreys ate their prey on the ground, I waited for Neptune to land on the shore and perch there, where I could procure the fish. He did not do me this courtesy, however, but instead circled me a few times, calling brashly, and finally flew onto my right shoulder to support his fish. This was not what I wanted. So I stretched my fist out to him, and he hopped on. Now the fish-lure served its purpose. My cousin held it in front of Neptune, covering up the real fish in the process. Neptune bobbed his head, but eventually still got on the lure and pecked at the little tidbits, while Herbert stowed the fish stealthily in the falconry bag.

So that was both the first success and failure. Success, because Neptune had finally caught prey in a true falconry fashion; failure, because he didn't give away his prey willingly, and he used me as a landing pad! So now I needed to train him out of these bad habits. I realized that ospreys in the wild didn't just use the ground to consume their prey, like their feathered hawk cousins, but also perched in trees near the water-line. In the absence of such a natural "dinner tree," Neptune used my shoulder, since I stood out from the flat shoreline. Recalling the tree we used to attract crows with an owl decoy, I found a thin tree roughly my height and placed it near the shoreline.

The following day we repeated the exercise with the barrel of fish, Neptune circled me again twice with the fish in tow, then flew straight to his new "tree" and settled there. I approached him quickly and took the fish in the same manner as the day before.

A few days later, on a warm, pretty summer day on which the fish especially enjoyed jumping, I returned to the pond with the osprey. This time there were no barrels or trapped fish. I strolled along the shore with Neptune, while he perched unconstrained on my fist. He looked with interest at the peaceful surface of the pond. Suddenly he reared up, began to dance in his characteristic fashion, then stooped and swished talons-first into the water. The surface roiled, and from the brief tumult Neptune ascended with a free-water fish. Drunk with victory, he let out a piercing yell and perched on his new tree. There I took the fish and let him hop on my hand.

Many hunts followed, rich with fish and ospreys. Today I can summarize my observations and experiences as follows:

Ospreys cannot be trained in the usual way for falcons and hawks, since his exclusive quarry is fish. He does not differentiate between carp, tench, pike or zander in the same way that a hawk speializes on a type of prey, like rabbits, and the osprey does not need to be retrained in the same way a falconer retrains the hawk to pursue pheasants. Ospreys can go without hoods, since stirred up wildlife does not disturb them, even less so humans or vehicles. You can also restrain ospreys with normal jesses while transporting them around the hunting area. If it is especially tame, you don't even need these "transport jesses," because it calmly perches on the glove or the roof rack of a car.

Ospreys do not just eat on the ground but prefer to eat in a tree near the shore. If no such tree is available, the raptor will use his falconer as a tree and settle down on his hat or shoulder. It is to a falconer's advantage to plant an appropriately sized tree near the shore where the osprey can bring his prey without too much difficulty. The osprey learns to hunt best with "release-fish" that are trapped in a barrel and that the handler can release into the pond at will. Every other method with fish- or bird-lures is pointless, because the osprey completely ignores any game on land. A fish-decoy or prepared fish is necessary to accustom the osprey to climbing onto the fist. If the osprey is especially well-trained, you can take away his catch without using any decoy, if you first cover the catch with your gloved hand while pulling it away with the other hand.

Ospreys are housed just like hawks or falcons in a mews with a tall perch. In front you should have a bath and a perch, but keep these under shade. Ospreys enjoy bathing more often than any other raptor.

It could be ecologically interesting to note that ospreys can coordinate their front talons as well as their rear talons individually, in order to tightly grasp their slippery prey. They carry their prey steadily with the head pointed in the direction of flight, never at an angle. In captivity they can only be fed with fresh fish, that ideally are enough that they can feed on it like a fish they caught themselves. The indigestible parts, like scales, bones, etc., they cast out as pellets.

The osprey usually stoops from the glove and returns there with its catch. So he "retrieves." This follows the custom of raptors to eat their prey on a high perch, where they are secure from egrets, that frequently try to steal their prey in wild environments. Now and then ospreys will stoop from high above the pond and then dive into the water with their talons first.

Sometimes the osprey underestimates the strength of their quarry. Then the falconer must haul out fish, osprey and all, with a large dip net, if he doesn't want to lose his bird. Birds of prey last only a little while under water.

I experienced nothing with nestlings or branchers (hunting with them would appear to be more difficult.) You can't follow an osprey into its hunting ground, but it will return to you after a successful catch. That is the fundamental difference between hunting for fish and other forms of falconry, hence my use of the term "retrieval."

The war interrupted my experiments with the osprey, and no possibility later presented itself of picking up the thread where it had been torn.

Every pond-keeper and fisherman should be informed that the harmfulness of ospreys is negligible, considering only a single bird. A breeding pair is a different matter, but breeding has not been documented in western Germany. Still, ospreys do not have canned goods. They hunt for self-sufficiency, and, many days, go with empty crops.

Whoever takes a utilitarian view of nature and only considers its material impact never comprehends the whole vastness and beauty of creation. Similarly, they will view my experiences and labors with the osprey as something useless and pointless, because it "produced" nothing.

But the observations and experiments with the osprey are experiences of nature's beauty. The noble flight and steep dive into the up-fountaining water enrich our knowledge of natural connections and teach us to care for ecological and biological balances, and to restore them where senseless and one-sided man-made policies have severely harmed them.

The osprey belongs to this nature and creation just like the fish and hawk, the rabbit and fox. Man needs to control himself, where necessary, with consideration for the biological circumstances and full attention for the creation, in which, at the end of the day, he is a first among equals and nothing else.

www.ingramcontent.com/pod-product-compliance
Lightning Source LLC
Chambersburg PA
CBHW050735030426
42336CB00012B/1583